KETTLEBELL TRAINING FOR ATHLETES

DEVELOP EXPLOSIVE POWER AND STRENGTH FOR MARTIAL ARTS, FOOTBALL, BASKETBALL, AND OTHER SPORTS

DAVE BELLOMO

PHOTOGRAPHY BY BRUCE CURTIS

New York   Chicago   San Francisco   Lisbon   London   Madrid   Mexico City
Milan   New Delhi   San Juan   Seoul   Singapore   Sydney   Toronto

The *McGraw·Hill* Companies

Copyright © 2010 by Dave Bellomo and Bruce Curtis. All rights reserved. Printed in the United States of America. Except as permitted under the United States Copyright Act of 1976, no part of this publication may be reproduced or distributed in any form or by any means, or stored in a database or retrieval system, without the prior written permission of the publisher.

2 3 4 5 6 7 8 9 10 11 12 13 14 15 16 17   DOC/DOC   1 9 8 7 6 5 4 3 2 1 0

ISBN   978-0-07-163588-2
MHID   0-07-163588-2

This book is for educational purposes. It is not intended as a substitute for individual fitness and health advice. Any use of the information in this book is at the reader's discretion. The author and publisher disclaim any and all liability arising directly or indirectly from the use or application of any information contained in this book.

Library of Congress Cataloging-in-Publication Data

Bellomo, Dave.
     Kettlebell training for athletes : develop explosive power and strength for martial
 arts, football, basketball, and other sports / Dave Bellomo.
          p.   cm.
     ISBN 0-07-163588-2
     1. Kettlebells.   2. Weight training.   I. Title.

 GV547.5.B45   2010
 613.7'13—dc22   2009052623

McGraw-Hill books are available at special quantity discounts to use as premiums and sales promotions or for use in corporate training programs. To contact a representative, please e-mail us at bulksales@mcgraw-hill.com.

This book is printed on acid-free paper.

Contents

WEEK 1:
BUILDING THE FOUNDATION
1

WEEK 2:
INTRODUCTION TO POWER MOVEMENTS
11

WEEK 3:
HEAVY HITTERS . . . BEEFING UP BALLISTICS
21

WEEK 4:
DEVELOPING COORDINATION AND RHYTHM   33
KETTLEBELLS WILL MAKE YOU A BETTER DANCER (NOT REALLY)

WEEK 5:
A QUICK CHANGE IN DIRECTION   45

WEEK 6:
COMBINATIONS   55
A DROPKICK TO YOUR WHOLE SYSTEM

GOAL SETTING

95

THE BIRTH OF THE BABY

SAMPLE PROGRAMS FOR
FOOTBALL AND SOCCER

115

SAMPLE PROGRAMS FOR
WRESTLING/GRAPPLING AND KARATE/
STRIKING SPORTS

129

SAMPLE PROGRAMS FOR
BASKETBALL AND BASEBALL

147

An Introduction to Kettlebells

Kettlebells have been around for more than a century. They were used extensively by the performing strongmen of the circuses during the late 1800s. Some strength historians will argue that kettlebells have existed for many centuries, dating back to when the Celts made them from stone. Whatever the case may be, kettlebells are making an amazing comeback in the strength and conditioning of athletes as well as in the everyday fitness programs of people around the world.

In recent years martial artists have been using kettlebells extensively in conditioning programs. These programs are designed to build strength and stamina without adding the unnecessary bulk of conventional bodybuilding programs. Also, the Russian sport of Girevoy has increased in popularity in those same circles. The object of Girevoy is to perform the highest number of repetitions you can with a fixed weight in the events of the clean and jerk (two kettlebells), the single snatch, and the single push-press. It is a very popular sport in Eastern Europe and has been growing in the United States as well.

Kettlebells, also called ring weights, come in many shapes and sizes. From cylinders to square blocks, the most common design resembles a cannonball with a handle on one side. This design has many advantages over the others, including the absence of sharp edges as well as an easier fit to the user's body.

These implements differ from dumbbells because the weight is distributed to one end rather than being even. This makes them ideal for performing ballistic, whole-body exercises such as cleans, snatches, and their variations. Kettlebells can be used either individually or in pairs. Unlike dumbbells, kettlebells are user friendly for performing movements such as the squat-pull because the weight distribution allows for comfort and correct body positioning.

These Old World weights are not just for the elite strongmen seen on television. Anyone who is healthy enough to strength train can learn to use kettlebells. Whether you are a great athlete or a great-grandmother, these simple tools will help you produce the most extraordinary results you have ever seen.

Kettlebell training is arguably the most effective and efficient form of strength training ever created. It is based upon whole-body, real-life movements that would be labeled as functional by today's so-called fitness experts. It is not that we are inventing this kind of training, only rediscovering it.

Fitness machines typically work in only one plane of movement, such as forward and backward or side to side. Many kettlebell exercises, however, incorporate movement into more than one plane, just as people move in real life. These implements can be used in a slow, controlled manner or explosively. They can be used to isolate a muscle, as well as for big, whole-body movements. Kettlebells are not only versatile but also extremely durable and cost-effective. They are so space efficient that they will even fit under your bed when you are finished with your workout.

My Kettlebell Journey

I first encountered kettlebell training when I enrolled in a sport judo program, approximately a decade ago. I like to refer to this period in my life as my early midlife crisis. I was too old for college-level sports programs, but I still had some competitive energy left in me. I figured that my background as a competitive powerlifter and my prior athletic experience would give me a huge advantage. I could not have been more wrong. Every class I took my first few months was the physical equivalent of being in a minor car wreck. I hurt everywhere and was getting very discouraged.

My wife saw me walk in my front door one night bleeding from my feet and hands and hobbling like I was a hundred years old. She asked, "Why are you doing this to yourself?"

My response was, in my trademarked stubborn tone, "I'm going through this until I am able to do this to someone else." It was really an artificially brave face. I was almost ready to quit.

Sensing I was unhappy with my progress, my instructor finally walked into my office and said, "You're strong, but you don't have the right kind of strength." After my ego recovered, I realized he was absolutely correct. There are many different types of strength, and each sport or task requires something different. I was strong for powerlifting. I had a strong press and a strong back and thighs to grind out a big squat, but I lacked explosiveness as well as twisting power in my trunk that was required for throwing. Also, my grip was strong, but I needed more strength in my fingers and more crushing strength to hold on to my opponents. I was very weak in the high-pull position, or pulling up from waist height to the chin, and it is critical in most major throws. Last, I was as slow as a three-legged tortoise in July.

The next time my instructor came over, he was carrying two kettlebells. He said, "Do you know what these are?"

"They're kettlebells," I replied. "What do you want me to do with them?" Being a fan of old-school strength training, I had seen them in books but had very little exposure to them.

"Lift them," he responded simply. He didn't like to elaborate too much or bore me with details. So with almost no instruction, I did. I must have come within an inch of breaking both wrists, my shin, and putting a hole in the floor. Little did I know these simple tools would completely redefine my training philosophy. At first I started to play around with the kettlebells, performing the few basic movements I had picked up. I tried single snatches, kettlebell sport cleans, presses, and rows. I was disappointed with my progress and decided not to bother with them for a while. They were light, fixed weights, and there was a learning curve to using them. Often, as students, we avoid things that are not easily learned only to find out that they are usually the most worthwhile of things to know.

A few months later I took a second look at the kettlebells. The tool was not the problem, but the limitations I had placed on how to use them were. I went back to the basics and asked myself what I wanted to accomplish. I, of course, wanted to be stronger, but I needed a much more functional strength that would allow me to pick up, twist, and turn much more effectively. I needed more explosiveness in whole-body movements. Power differs from strength because it includes the element of time. To become more powerful, I needed to add speed to my strength and teach the muscles of my body to work together as efficiently as possible. I also needed stamina. I never had much luck running, and other forms of cardio bored me to tears. "Now we're getting somewhere," I thought.

I looked at the kettlebells. They were 35 and 50 pounds, respectively—a bit too light for my taste. I wanted something heavy enough so I would feel like I was actually grappling with an opponent. I asked a friend of mine if he could make me something heavier. He said he could, but not to expect anything uniform or exact. What I ended up with was a slightly irregular ball of iron with a handle. It weighed a total of 66 pounds, and it was beautiful.

Next I looked at the exercises I had previously performed and decided they did not have enough relevance to my goals. I needed to come up with my own movements that would give me the type of strength I wanted in the motor patterns that I needed to practice. Performing a concentration curl would have less value to me than a whole-body movement that included pulling, pressing, and an explosive extension of the hips and knees. I wanted the kind of strength and power that would enable me to grab a grown man and rip him off of his feet using one hand. I am not that big of a guy, so I definitely set my sights high.

I tried to forget what I thought I knew about strength training and to start over. I took the skills that I needed to perform and deconstructed them into their basic elements. I started with the clean. I liked the ballistic element of barbell power and hang cleans, but I needed something that I could perform both with one and two hands. Also, I needed to include some rotation of the trunk to more closely simulate grappling. Last, the exercise needed to be not only powerful, but also something that could be repeated as many times as my stamina would allow.

Conventional types of barbell cleans didn't have the trunk rotation I needed nor did they have the ability to be safely performed with one hand or for many repetitions. Dumbbell cleans lacked the feel of grappling and didn't have the right weight distribution. Dumbbells are weighted on both ends, and as one end comes up, it is pulled along by the other end coming down. This doesn't allow for a smooth pull. Again, I was back to kettlebells.

I examined the kettlebell sport clean that I had learned previously. It is a great exercise consisting of a type of shoulder-width stand-up, followed by dipping back down, and looping the kettlebell around your shoulder. As a stand-alone exercise, this clean variation works many big muscle groups and is great for explosion and stamina. It didn't, however, give me the pulling power I sought nor did it give me the larger range of motion I was looking for. What I did then was to create a version of the clean that worked for me. That is the beauty of kettlebells. They are so versatile that you can do few things that are absolutely wrong. There only are techniques that are more appropriate than others for a given task.

The clean that I developed was more of a high-pull than a pull over the shoulder. In my mind I would think "grip and rip." Grip the handle tight, and rip it off of the floor. I would imagine grabbing my opponent's gi (a martial arts uniform) and pulling him right off of his feet. It took a little work to smoothen it out, but this is the technique that I teach my students to this day. I changed other movements to make them suit my needs, and I left others alone. Whatever your goals are, though, one thing is for sure: kettlebells are extremely effective training tools and will transform your strengthening and conditioning program.

Getting Started

To get started in kettlebell training, you really need only a strong desire to better yourself and a kettlebell of appropriate weight. However, a few things will make your kettlebell quest go a little smoother:

1. Make sure you are in good health and that it is OK for you to pursue a vigorous exercise program.
2. Make sure you have sufficient space if you are training inside (although outdoor training is great). You will want at least a 6-foot-by-6-foot area that is slightly higher than arm's length overhead.
3. A rubber mat is a good investment and will help prevent damage to your floor.
4. Some loose clothing such as sweatpants or shorts and a T-shirt are good for comfort and range of motion.
5. You will need some kettlebells.

PURCHASING A KETTLEBELL

Kettlebells come in all shapes and sizes. The most common form you see today is a ball with a handle. Some are hollow, and their weight can be adjusted. Others are solid and of fixed weight. I prefer fixed weights, personally. If you can afford it, start with at least two kettlebells of different weights. Most average male athletes will start with 35-pound and 50-pound weights or 50-pound and 65-pound weights. Women usually start with 15-pound and 25-pound weights or 25-pound and 35-pound weights. These are just very rough guidelines, and you should go with the weights you are most comfortable using, because you can always progress in weight later. When you are able to perform single movements with the heavier of your two kettlebells, you may want to consider buying a third kettlebell that is equivalent in weight to your lighter one. Now you will be able to do double work, or kettlebell exercises that require two kettlebells, such as double cleans, double snatches, alternating cleans, double presses, double rows, and so on. Over time your kettlebell collection will grow, as will your strength, and you will end up passing these durable tools of physical development on to others. A kettlebell really is an entire health club packed into a little iron ball.

POSTURE AND BREATHING

I am frequently asked, "When should I breathe?" There are different schools of thought regarding breathing. Some coaches say to inhale on the upswing of a snatch. Other coaches say to always exhale when you are exerting, which contradicts the prior statement. A case can be made for both. You definitely do not, however, want to hold your breath throughout a set. You will get light-headed and be at an increased risk for injury. What I tell my clients is to just breathe. You will find a rhythm that works for you. Just make sure that every repetition receives one full breath. Whether you inhale or exhale going up is less important than breathing smoothly and regularly.

LEARN BY DOING

The best way to learn how to use kettlebells is by training with them. This book is organized into an eight-week workout plan. It is designed to introduce you to the basic elements of kettlebell training week by week. With each set of new exercises, photographs show the critical points of each movement. At the end of the exercise descriptions, each exercise has a Key Points section that reviews the exercise technique. This repetition helps you remember the major steps of each kettlebell exercise. Following all of the exercise descriptions are more kettlebell exercises, as well as sections on program design and sample routines. This, along with a kettlebell, is everything that you need to get started. With proper technique and lots of hard work, you can transform your workouts and make progress that you never thought possible.

Work out with each exercise list, three nonconsecutive days per week to start. Perform each exercise for 3 to 5 repetitions. Take as long as you need for a rest break between exercises. Work through each list of exercises three to five times, top to bottom. Gradually add repetitions, weight, or both, but always keep technique as your top priority. Practice makes permanent, so make sure you are practicing perfect form.

When you have completed this eight-week kettlebell program, you will have developed the foundation for all of your future training. The first eight weeks are meant to teach you the fundamental kettlebell movements that all the major movements are based on. This period is also meant to condition your body for the next training phase—something that every good program does.

The next step is to decide how you would like to proceed. You need to think beyond the first eight weeks. As your strength and skill improve, so should your program. Kettlebell training allows for adaptation and flexibility like no other. You need to set goals and map out a plan. If you have a specific sport in mind, you can use one of the sample programs explained later in this book or you can start completely from scratch. The choice is yours.

Ultimately, each program must be fine-tuned to meet the specific needs and characteristics of the athlete using it. What works for one person might not work exactly the same way for another, so feel free to experiment to find out what works best for you. Choose a direction of training that will most benefit your particular sport, such as strength, power, endurance, or a specific combination of these traits. Simply start within a modest range of intensity and volume; then gradually challenge yourself as your body adapts. You will be amazed at what levels of physical and mental stress you will be able to tolerate. These small but permanent changes will add up to great sums of work over time and will, without question, greatly improve your sports performance.

BUILDING THE FOUNDATION

In this chapter you will learn the small yet critical point that whole-body explosiveness is based upon: the ability to channel momentum through the body by coordinating the extension of the knee and hip. These two joints must be activated as efficiently as possible for any of the ballistic movements to be performed correctly.

The deadlift is the simplest example of this. It forces you into the body position that you will use for all of the major movements. I sometimes refer to this as the linebacker position. Like a linebacker, you want to have a balanced stance with your shoulders, knees, and feet stacked over each other. You want to look straight ahead or up slightly because, very simply, you lean where you look.

From the deadlift you move on to the squat-pull. It is an extension of the deadlift and incorporates many muscle groups of the upper body. It teaches you to take the power you have developed from the floor and channel it into the muscles of your upper body. Eventually you learn to then transfer this power into a sporting object like a shot for the shot put or into an opponent such as during a wrestling match.

Next, the two-hand swing is your introduction to the ballistic movements. It is simple, yet extremely effective. It teaches you how to take the positioning of the deadlift and add explosiveness through the thighs, hips, and back. Regardless of how you have trained in the past or will train in the future, the power gained from the swing is always a great addition to any program.

Last are the two meat-and-potatoes upper-body exercises of the bent-over row and the two-hand press. These balance out the whole-body workout. I have found over the years that the more my training advances, the more I use the most basic exercises. The row and the two-hand press cover most of the major muscles of the upper body and give strength for the more advanced movements that require a level of balance.

Deadlift

The deadlift is an exercise that uses the big muscles of the thighs, hips, and lower back. It is basically a pickup from the floor. This exercise allows you to practice your posture for the ballistic movements that will come later in this book.

Straddle the kettlebell with your toes lining up with the handle. Your feet should be slightly wider that your shoulders and pointed outward slightly. Looking straight ahead, bend your knees slightly and then bend your hips. This allows you to keep your back in the proper alignment. As you drop your hips, keep the muscles that run along your spine contracted. This aids in stabilizing your back and keeping you safe during this exercise. You want a flat, relatively straight back. Grab the kettlebell, drive off of the floor, and stand up into a fully erect position. Repeat this sequence of movements, while maintaining a tight grip on the handle, until your set is completed. Continue to focus on your posture throughout the set.

DEADLIFT: KEY POINTS

1. Straddle the kettlebell.
2. Line your toes up with the handle.
3. Place your feet slightly wider than your shoulders and pointed out.
4. Look straight ahead.
5. Keep your spinal erectors tight.
6. Bend your knees and then your hips, and drop into a squatting position.
7. Drive off of the floor with your hips, thighs, and lower back, and stand up into erect position.

Deadlift   In the deadlift, posture is everything. Here you learn how to squat down while maintaining a flat back. The posture you develop here will either help or hinder all of your future kettlebell training.

Squat-Pull

The squat-pull, also called the high pull, is one of my all-time favorite exercises. It uses most of the major muscle groups of the body, including those of the thighs, hips, lower back, upper back, and shoulders. This is great for football players, wrestlers, and martial artists because it combines the pulling motion of the arms with the explosive extension of the knees and hips. This combination of motions is critical for the major techniques of many sports.

The setup of the squat-pull is identical to that of the dead-lift. Line up your toes with the handle, feet slightly wider than shoulder-width apart and pointed slightly outward. Keeping your head up and your shoulders back, drop down and grab the weight. As you drive upward and extend your knees and

Squat-Pull The squat-pull starts out with the linebacker-like stance. The hips are low, the head is up, and the back is flat. As you explode from the bottom, draw the kettlebell up your body. It should be in constant contact with your body from your waist to your chest and back down again. As you draw it up to your chest, pull your elbows into a V as you would for an upright row. This brings your deltoids into play and saves your wrists unnecessary strain.

your hips, continue the movement by drawing your hands up your body toward your chin. This part of the movement looks like an upright row. Keep your elbows turned up and slightly higher than your hands to avoid injuring your wrists. To lower the kettlebell, allow your arms to fully extend toward the floor before you start to bend your knees and hips. Also, remember to let your legs do most of the work.

SQUAT-PULL: KEY POINTS

1. Set up the same way as for the deadlift.
2. Stand up to the erect position just as for the deadlift.
3. Continue movement by bending your elbows and drawing your hands upward toward your chin.
4. Keep your elbows turned up higher than your hands.
5. Let your arms fully extend on the way down before bending your knees and hips.
6. Just before hitting the floor, visualize hitting a spring and drive back up for the next repetition.

Caution: When raising the kettlebell, do not allow your hands to reach your chin, to avoid contact between your chin and the handle.

Two-Hand Swing

As with all the major power movements, line up your feet with the kettlebell as you would for the deadlift. My preferred technique for this movement is to stand up as you would in a deadlift and then lower your hips so your hands are even with your knees. This is helps you get into the correct posture. Next, swing the weight backward through your knees to gain some momentum. This is called a backswing and is referenced throughout this book. When the kettlebell reaches a natural apex and your forearms are just beginning to brush against your thighs, forcefully extend your knees and hips and explode upward. The momentum you generate by pushing off of the ground transfers into the weight. Gently follow through with the arms and shoulders until the kettlebell is at eye level. Your arms should be straight out from your body with the kettlebell lined up perfectly with

Two-Hand Swing As you can see from the photographs of the previous two exercises, most major kettlebell exercises are connected. Almost all of the major kettlebell movements start in or go through the basic linebacker stance. Here once again is the crouched, flat-backed position. The head is up, and the eyes are looking straight ahead or slightly up. You want to start the weight moving backward (the "backswing") before you bring it up to eye level; otherwise, you will place unnecessary stress on your shoulders trying to front-raise a large weight. Also, as the weight moves forward, you want to stand fully erect with straight knees and hips. This allows you to transfer all of the momentum that you gained from the swing into the kettlebell.

your forearms. Let gravity pull the kettlebell toward the floor and swing back between your legs. Bounce it back up for the next repetition. If executed properly, this ballistic exercise will be felt in the muscles of the thighs, hips, lower back, upper back, and shoulders, not in the joints. Remember to keep your head up and shoulders back.

TWO-HAND SWING: KEY POINTS

1. Straddle the weight with your feet slightly wider than your shoulders.
2. Line your toes up with the handle.
3. Get into the squatting position with your back and feet flat.
4. Grab the kettlebell with both hands.
5. Keep your eyes directed straight ahead.
6. Stand up with the weight to get into position.
7. Slowly lower the kettlebell until it is even with your knees.
8. Swing backward to gain momentum.
9. Drive from your hips, thighs, and lower back.
10. Follow through with your shoulders until the kettlebell is at eye level. The kettlebell should be an extension of your body and lined up evenly with your arms.
11. Let gravity pull the kettlebell down between your legs.
12. Bounce the kettlebell back up for the next repetition.

Bent-Over Row

This is the first major movement dedicated to the upper back. As the name implies, this is a pull, or row, in the bent-over position. It can be performed with a variety of grips and stances. For now, however, use standard foot and hand positioning. Place the kettlebell even with your front foot. The handle should be parallel with your foot. Step back with your opposite leg slightly farther than a normal stride. Again, your foot should be parallel to the kettlebell handle. Brace yourself by placing the hand of your forward side on your thigh. Bend at your waist so that your upper body is almost parallel to the ground. Grab the kettlebell with your free hand, and pull the handle to your ribs without twisting your upper body. Lower the kettlebell almost to the floor, and repeat for the next repetition. When you are finished with your set on one side, reverse your position and repeat on the other.

Bent-Over Row   Both feet are pointed straight ahead to align the hips and shoulders. Also, the body position is fairly low so you can place the majority of the stress on the large upper-back muscles. A higher body position will turn a bent-over row into an upright row for the shoulders. Remember, body low, feet straight, shoulders and hips aligned.

BENT-OVER ROW: KEY POINTS

1. Stagger your step approximately a stride's length so your feet are pointing straight ahead and are parallel.
2. Bend at the waist, and brace yourself by placing your forward hand on your thigh.
3. Grip the kettlebell with your free hand, and pull to your ribs without twisting your upper body.
4. Lower the kettlebell almost to the floor, and repeat.

Two-Hand Press

There are many variations of the overhead press. The two-hand press is a good one to start with because it requires a bit less balance than some of the others. It gives you a chance to build up your confidence so you can try some of the others later. Grip the kettlebell on its sides with your thumbs wrapped tightly around the handle. The handle should be resting on the top of your chest. Your hands should be underneath it, and the handle should be parallel to the ground. Bend your knees slightly to keep excessive strain off of your low back. Keeping your eyes level, press the kettlebell straight over your head. Pause briefly at the top; then slowly lower the kettlebell down to your chest.

TWO-HAND PRESS: KEY POINTS

1. Hold the kettlebell by its sides so the handle is resting on your chest and your thumbs are wrapped around it.
2. Bend your knees slightly.
3. Keep your eyes level, and press the kettlebell straight overhead.
4. Pause briefly; then slowly lower the kettlebell to your chest.

Two-Hand Press   Note the placement of the kettlebell high on the chest. You want to keep your elbows tucked underneath your hands to create a base of support for the weight. The natural tendency is to flare the elbows and let the kettlebell slide down. This mistake, however, places an unnecessary stress on the shoulders and back of the neck and will cause premature fatigue.

INTRODUCTION TO POWER MOVEMENTS

This chapter discusses the one-hand swing, single snatch, double clean, and single press. The one-hand swing is the next progression in the ballistic movements. I find that it takes slightly more coordination than the two-hand swing for two reasons: First, you must lean away from the weight slightly to keep it centered. Second, the tendency when progressing from two hands to one is to activate more muscle in the shoulder. But the true power in the movement still comes from the hips. I tell my clients to drive from the hips and try to relax the shoulder as much as they can. You need a bit more upper-body strength for the one-hand swing than for the two-hand swing—not twice as much, however, just slightly more. The main drive still comes from the muscles of the lower body when they are working together.

Next are the monster movements of the snatch and double clean. These are two of the most explosive exercises out there. The single snatch is considered one of, if not *the*, greatest exercises by kettlebell practitioners in terms of overall benefit. It necessitates a very large range of motion that goes from the floor to full extension overhead, using almost all the major muscle groups in the body. Using this much muscle at once places a very great demand on the cardiovascular system. This alone makes the single snatch a great exercise. The large range of motion also requires a very high level of explosiveness. You must commit to the snatch from the very bottom of the range and drive through until reaching the top. There is no halfway in the snatch: either you put it overhead, or you get out of the way.

The double clean is the first of what I like to call heavy ballistics, or power movements that might use a large amount of weight or intensity. It involves a short range of motion that comes from the knees up, similar to that of a hang clean with a barbell. It uses two kettlebells at once but is still user friendly because the body alignment is straight rather than leaning to one side. You use a fairly wide stance to clear the weights, which further reduces the range of motion, but you can use fairly heavy kettlebells because such large muscle groups are coming into play.

Last, this week includes the single press. Like its cousin, the two-hand press, the single press is a great exercise for the chest, shoulders, and triceps. Unlike the two-hand press, however, the single press requires more balance in the shoulder and more stability in the trunk. During the single press you need to lean quite far, away from the kettlebell, to maintain proper body alignment. You start with a wide stance. When the kettlebell is at full extension, you should be able to draw a line from the weight to the center of your base. This positioning requires a strong midsection and is great for overall development of the upper-body muscles.

One-Hand Swing

As the name states, this movement is very similar to the two-hand swing. There are some subtle differences, however. Regarding posture and foot placement, set up the same way you would for a two-hand swing. When you grip the handle with one hand, make sure to center the kettlebell between your legs by leaning slightly to the side. Start with the same backswing as you would for the two-hand swing. Then drive the kettlebell forward and up with your hips and thighs. Gently follow through with your shoulder until the kettlebell reaches eye level. When the kettlebell reaches eye level, let gravity bring it back down between your knees. Remember to continue to center the kettlebell throughout the movement. Repeat with your opposite hand.

One-Hand Swing   The positioning for the one-hand swing is the same as for the two-hand swing, with two exceptions. First and most obvious, the grip is with one hand instead of two. Second, to center the kettlebell between the knees, you have to lean slightly away from it. The swing pattern still needs to follow the midline of the body, whether you are using one hand or two.

ONE-HAND SWING: KEY POINTS

1. Set up as you would for a two-hand swing.
2. Keep the kettlebell centered.
3. Drive from your hips, thighs, and lower back.
4. Follow through with your shoulder until the kettlebell is at eye level.
5. Let gravity pull the kettlebell down for the next repetition.

Single Snatch

Kettlebell practitioners consider the single snatch to be one of the greatest and most beneficial kettlebell movements. It has a huge range of motion that goes from the floor to arm's length overhead and uses almost all of the major muscle groups. It also demands an extremely explosive execution that will translate to most sports.

Again, start with the basic setup of the deadlift and swing. Just as with the single swing, take a large backswing to get the kettlebell moving. Unlike the swing, however, the snatch has to come overhead for a full lockout. This means you have to generate significantly more power than you would for a swing that is going only to eye level. This explosion must begin at the bottom of the movement if you are to successfully complete the snatch. Also, you need to continue to drive and follow through with your whole body throughout the entire range of motion. Last, you need to get the kettlebell to gently roll onto your forearm by pushing into the handle approximately 12 inches before you reach the top of the movement. This starts the handle turning under the kettlebell and makes for a soft landing.

This sounds extremely confusing and borderline insane, but it is not as complicated as it sounds and will be well worth your effort. When snatches are performed correctly, they are very smooth and fluid and have almost no impact on the forearm. It takes a little practice to get the feel of this movement.

Single Snatch   The single snatch is basically a single swing that has been followed through into an overhead lockout. Understand that more force is needed to complete the larger range of motion. Also, remember to push into the weight just before lockout so the kettlebell rolls onto your forearm instead of slamming into it.

SINGLE SNATCH: KEY POINTS

1. Set up the same way as you would for the single swing.
2. Use a big backswing to gain momentum.
3. Be explosive throughout the entire movement.
4. Follow through with your shoulder, and drive past eye level.
5. Push into the kettlebell just before the top of the movement so the handle goes under the ball and the kettlebell gently rolls onto your forearm.

Double Clean

There are several variations of the clean, and the double clean is the easiest to begin with. Simply put, a clean is a pull to a racked position on the shoulder. Double cleans are easier to learn than single cleans because the body is upright and symmetrical. You therefore do not have to lean to the side as you would for a single clean.

Double Clean Think of the double clean as a swing until the weight reaches waist height. At that point, tuck your elbows in and let them glide over the outside of your shoulders. Note that the weights are situated fairly low on the model's shoulders. This is to keep unnecessary stress off of the muscles of the rotator cuff. The double kettlebell clean is more closely related to a kettlebell swing than a barbell clean, where the elbows are up and the bar is on the shoulders in the racked, or top, position.

First, line up two kettlebells so that the handles are in a straight line. Straddle the kettlebells, and line your toes up with the handles. You want your legs wide enough apart to clear the weights but not so wide that you feel off balance. Keeping your head up and shoulders back, start your backswing. As you swing both kettlebells forward, pull your elbows into your sides and begin to move your hands to the outside of your shoulders. This is the same movement you would use to open a coat. As you flip the kettlebells over, natural shelves are created with your hands, elbows, and shoulders. Once the kettlebells are in the racked position, pause briefly and then tip your elbows up. This allows you to direct the kettlebells. Allow the weights to swing between your knees, stretching the back, hips, and thighs; then bring them up for the next clean.

DOUBLE CLEAN: KEY POINTS

1. Line the kettlebells up with their handles in a straight line.

2. Straddle both kettlebells.

3. Start with the backswing; then bring the kettlebells forward.

4. Pull your elbows into your sides.

5. Move your hands outward like you would to open a coat.

6. Flip the kettlebells over onto the sides of your upper arms.

7. Pause briefly; then tip your elbows up to direct the kettlebells back between your knees for the next repetition.

Single Press

The next pressing exercise you will add to your arsenal is the single press. Start with a moderate weight. Bring it to the outside of your upper arm. Take a fairly wide stance, and turn your head so you can look at the weight. This helps you keep your balance. The elbow of your active arm should be tucked into your side. Brace your stationary hand against your hip. Lean slightly away from the kettlebell so your hip helps support the weight. Press to full extension. If your body is properly aligned, you can draw an imaginary line from the kettlebell to the center of your stance. Pause briefly; then slowly lower the weight until your elbow is once again tucked into your side.

Single Press   Note that the model is leaning to one side and the hip is pushed out to the side of the weighted hand. This gives extra support to the weight and takes the main stress off of the lower back muscles. When the weight is pressed upward, you should be able to draw a line from the kettlebell directly down between the feet.

SINGLE PRESS: KEY POINTS

1. Start with the kettlebell on the outside of your upper arm with your elbow tucked into your side.
2. Widen your stance to greater than shoulder width.
3. Turn your head, and look at the weight for balance.
4. Press to a full extension.
5. The kettlebell should be directly over the center of your stance.
6. Slowly lower the kettlebell until your elbow is tucked into your side.

HEAVY HITTERS . . . BEEFING UP BALLISTICS

Chapter 3 continues heavy ballistic training with the single clean, double snatch, and sidewinder. It then finishes with the extremely effective movements of the side shuffle and double press.

The single clean is probably my all-time favorite kettlebell movement. When performed with heavy weight, the single clean packs a punch for most of the body. I created this variation of the clean for grappling sports, though it works great for any athlete who needs a great deal of pulling power and hip explosiveness. This might include rowers, climbers, football players, or strongmen. It is also brutal in developing grip strength, an often overlooked aspect of athletic performance. This variation requires the athlete to grip a heavy weight with one hand, pull it off of the floor, and then rotate it over the side of the shoulder while leaning to the other side. It is somewhat like slinging a large duffle bag over the shoulder, except in this case the duffle bag could weigh as much as a person.

The double snatch is one of the toughest exercises in terms of the amount of power required to execute it, as well as the overall shock to the body. It is similar to the single snatch, except that it is double the fun, requiring two kettlebells. It requires an extra step in lowering the weight. The double snatch demands that the athlete be totally committed to the execution of this exercise. There is no partially completed repetition for this exercise—only success or failure, where failure might result in injury. When performing this movement, concentrate fully on proper technique and give 100 percent from the very beginning. Otherwise you might get caught halfway through the range of motion with two kettlebells in your hands and no chance of locking them out.

In the lowering portion of the double snatch, I like to include the extra step of lowering the kettlebells to the shoulders and then taking them back down either to the floor or between the knees for the next repetition. This keeps the kettlebells from pulling you forward, which is somewhat likely with the combined weight of the kettlebells, large range of motion, and awkward body positioning. I actually picked this step up at a clinic I hosted many years ago, where I mentioned the problem of balance with the double snatch. One of the more advanced participants brought this innovative technique to my attention, and I have been using it ever since.

The sidewinder is a squat-pull variation. It reminds me of a double leg takedown in wrestling; in fact, it is quite often included in programs I develop for wrestlers. The athlete starts the same as for a squat-pull, and then leans to one side, scooping the kettlebell up into the opposite underarm. This can be repeated for one side or alternated, which is my preference. The sidewinder gives you pickup strength in the lower body but adds an upper-body pull and trunk development as well. In addition, it teaches you lateral movement in the upper body.

Like the sidewinder, the side shuffle teaches the athlete how to move laterally with weight. It can be performed on an aerobic step, a block, or the floor. In this movement, you begin in a crouched position. Ankles, knees, hips, and elbows are all bent, and the feet are almost touching. You take a large step to the side with one foot and then point the kettlebell to just inside that ankle. This creates a stretch along the groin, hamstring, and buttock of that leg. You then quickly push back to center and shuffle to repeat the movement on the other side. Back and forth you go with speed and quickness. Very little time at all should be spent in any one of the three positions. You should be constantly in movement. The side shuffle is excellent for any sport requiring lateral movement. This would include sports such as basketball, soccer, grappling sports, football, and both field and ice hockey.

Last, this chapter includes the double press. It is a tough upper-body movement because you aren't given any breaks and you are forced to press in a large range of motion due to your upright stance. You also are using two kettlebells, so your shoulder balance and stability are tested as well. This exercise could be performed with dumbbells, but they do not give you the complete range of motion that kettlebells do. When pressing with kettlebells, you actually bring your hands to the front of your shoulders and get a deeper stretch than with dumbbells, because the weight is on the outside of your forearm and therefore not inhibiting the range in any way. Also, because of the position of the kettlebells against the arms, you have to be constantly pulling the kettlebells in to keep the weights from falling to the sides. This job goes primarily to the anterior deltoids and the pectoral muscles and adds further challenge to this exercise. You will find yourself starting with lighter weights than if you were using dumbbells.

Single Clean

The single clean is arguably the most difficult of the clean variations to learn. It is, however, well worth your effort because it translates beautifully to sports such as football, wrestling, judo, and jujitsu. I developed this particular style of clean for grappling sports in particular. Remember, a clean is a pull to a racked position on the outside of the upper arm and shoulder.

Start as you would for a one-hand swing. As the kettlebell swings forward, pull your elbow back into your side. Just as

Single Clean Note that the setup for the single clean is the same for the one-hand swing as well as the single snatch. Also, view how the hip of the model presses toward the kettlebell to give extra support just as in the setup for the single press. Kettlebell training can be reduced to a handful of body alignments. The lesson here is to be efficient.

the kettlebell begins to flip over your elbow, lean to the side away from it. This pushes your hip out, which helps support the weight. The kettlebell should land smoothly in the racked position. As the kettlebell begins to make contact with your body, bend your knees slightly to absorb some of the shock. Pause briefly, and then tip your elbow up to direct the kettlebell down for the next repetition.

SINGLE CLEAN: KEY POINTS

1. Set up as you would for a single swing.
2. Pull your elbow to your side as the kettlebell reaches waist height.
3. Lean away from the kettlebell as it flips over your elbow.
4. Rack the kettlebell on the outside of your upper arm and shoulder. Do not allow your hand to go past your shoulder in the rack position.
5. Slightly bend your knees to absorb shock as the kettlebell comes into contact with your body.
6. Tip your elbow to direct the weight toward the floor for the next repetition.

Double Snatch

The double snatch is performed with two kettlebells. Set up as you would for a double clean. Keeping your head up and your shoulders back, take a big backswing. Explode forcefully from the bottom, and drive with your whole body. When the kettlebells are approximately 12 inches from the top position, push into the handles as you would for a single snatch. When executed properly, there is very little impact on the forearms. At this point, lower the kettlebells to your shoulders, and then tip your elbows to direct the kettlebells downward. This step keeps you from being set off-balance by the weights. Swing the kettlebell between your knees, and explode back up for the next repetition.

Double Snatch   The flat back and correct posture in the beginning of the double snatch make all the difference in the success of this movement. Note that at midpoint, the knees and hips are extended to transfer the momentum gained in the bottom position to the lockout. At the endpoint of the movement, the weights are fully extended overhead and are properly aligned with the body's base of support.

DOUBLE SNATCH: KEY POINTS

1. Set up as you would for the double clean.
2. Use a strong backswing.
3. Snatch both kettlebells as you would for a single snatch.
4. Push into the kettlebells 12 inches before the top of the movement.
5. Lower the kettlebells to the shoulders before tipping down into the next repetition.

Sidewinder

The sidewinder is a variation of the squat-pull discussed earlier in this book. It is a great exercise for grappling sports like wrestling because it will assist you when drilling pickups, as well as single- and double-leg takedowns. Also, you just may want to use this variation to spice up a stale routine.

Sidewinder   Again, the beginning sidewinder position resembles the starting positions of the swings and cleans. It is basically a squat-pull to the side. To get any weight to move, the knees and hips need to be quickly extended. This brings you back to the basic deadlift, or linebacker position as I call it.

Begin by setting up as you would for a squat-pull. As you extend your knees and hips, lean away from the kettlebell to one side. At this point, pull with your top arm, bending your elbow farther. As you lower the weight, center your trunk once again. Explode out of the bottom position, and repeat with the other side. Continue to alternate sides until your set is complete.

SIDEWINDER: KEY POINTS

1. Set up the same way as for the squat-pull.
2. Extend your knees and hips, and begin pulling the kettlebell toward your chin.
3. Lean to one side, away from the kettlebell.
4. Continue pulling with your top elbow.
5. Center up as you lower the weight.
6. Switch sides as you drive up for the next repetition.

Side Shuffle

Very few exercises prepare you to move laterally, yet most major sports such as football, basketball, and soccer require almost constant lateral movement. To help prepare athletes for a quick change in direction, a friend and I developed what we call the side shuffle. This can be performed over a step, over a low bench, or flat on the floor. Begin by holding the kettlebell with both hands. Bring your feet together, and bend your elbows and your knees. This puts you into a sort of crouching position. Extend one leg straight out to the side, slightly farther than a normal stride. Follow that with your arms so you are pointing the kettlebell at the space just inside your ankle. Next pull your arms and leg to the center, and repeat with the opposite side. The transition from side to side should be a quick gliding motion. As your technique improves, pick up your speed.

SIDE SHUFFLE: KEY POINTS

1. Hold the handle with both hands.
2. Bring your feet close together.
3. Bend your elbows, waist, and knees.
4. Extend one leg straight out to the side.
5. Follow that leg with your arms, pointing the kettlebell to the inside of your ankle.
6. Pull your arms and leg to center, and repeat on the opposite side.
7. Transitioning from side to side should be a quick gliding motion.

Side Shuffle   To perform the side shuffle, start in a sort of crouched position with elbows and knees bent. Think of a hockey player sprinting down the ice. When you push off to the side, you lunge as deeply as you can and then shuffle through the midpoint of the exercise to the other side.

Double Press

Clean the kettlebells to the outside of your shoulders. Bend your knees slightly, and tighten your stomach to stabilize your lower back. Looking straight ahead, press the kettlebells overhead with your arms fully extended. Pause briefly, and then lower the kettlebells until they are once again on the sides of your shoulders. Your elbows should be tucked into your sides.

Double Press   To maximize the range of motion of the double press, you should start in the top position of the double clean if possible. This gives you up to 6 additional inches of range and allows for a much fuller development of the shoulders. When pressing the kettlebells, extend your arms completely overhead. The kettlebells should be directly over the middle of your feet and not leaning to the front.

DOUBLE PRESS VARIATION: PUSH-PRESS

If you feel like trying slightly heavier weights, you can add a push with your legs. This would simply be called a push-press. For this technique, begin by bending your knees and pressing your feet into the floor to gain momentum. The push-press is sometimes used to prepare for the next weight advancement in the press.

DOUBLE PRESS: KEY POINTS

1. Clean the kettlebells to the sides of your shoulders.
2. Look straight head, tighten your abdominal muscles, and slightly bend your knees.
3. Press to full extension.
4. Pause briefly at the top; then slowly lower the weights until the kettlebells are in the starting position.

DEVELOPING COORDINATION AND RHYTHM

KETTLEBELLS WILL MAKE YOU A BETTER DANCER (NOT REALLY)

This chapter will challenge your grip and coordination with exercises such as double swings, alternating cleans, double rows, and the one-stays-up press. The chapter also features double squats, which are big thigh builders, and the single floor press, which develops the muscles of the chest, shoulder, and back of the arm.

The chapter begins with the double swing. This very simple exercise is brutally effective for developing overall strength and power. It challenges your grip as well as your balance. You have to fight to hang on to both weights and to keep from being pulled forward by them. The lesson with this movement is to plant your feet and to not let the kettlebells get out of your control even for an instant.

Alternating cleans have a range of motion similar to that of the double clean. When being performed, they require a rhythm that is unlike other kettlebell exercises. The alternating clean is great for developing explosiveness in the hips as well as developing upper-body pulling power because of its short range of motion. You probably want to start out with a light weight for this one until you get your timing down. It also taxes your grip and forearms, so be prepared for sore muscles if you have been neglecting your grip.

Double rows and the one-stays-up press will both challenge your balance more than you think. The double row requires you to stay almost parallel to the ground and forces you to sit back toward your heels. The one-stays-up press will have you pressing one kettlebell at a time while keeping another kettlebell fully extended overhead at all times. This means that the muscles of your legs, trunk, and shoulders have to be engaged for balance throughout the entire set. Also, the prime movers as well as the stabilizing muscles of each shoulder will be taxed to the max.

Double squats and single floor presses round out the lineup. Both are excellent exercises and give you basic, foundational strength. Double squats probably do not allow you to train as heavily as you would normally with barbell squats; however, they challenge you with a deep range of motion and the ability to alter your stance. This lets you emphasize specific areas of your lower body and change positions without setting your weights down. The single floor press is a simple chest and shoulder exercise with a twist. You have to use your abdominal muscles to keep from getting pulled to one side. Even if you use your free arm for a counterbalance, you still feel the muscles of your trunk coming into play.

Double Swing

As the name indicates, this swing uses two kettlebells at once. This great exercise challenges your grip, although usually I prefer using one heavier kettlebell. The double swing is a good exercise to perform when a single heavy kettlebell is not available or you simply want to add variety to your routine.

Set up as you would for a double clean. Make your stance wide enough for the kettlebells to pass between your legs. An excessively wide stance, however, will throw you off-balance.

Double Swing   Set up in the same way as you would for any of the big ballistic movements. Regardless of weight, posture must be perfect in the setup. Drive from the hips, and allow the kettlebells to become an extension of your body. Make sure that for the double swing you are balanced so you are not pulled forward.

Keeping your head up and your shoulders back, start with a strong backswing to get the kettlebells moving. Extend your knees and hips, and drive the kettlebells forward. Stand up into a fully erect position, and follow through with the swing until the kettlebells reach eye level. Let gravity bring them down between your knees. Allow the kettlebells to pass between your legs. Continue to look straight ahead, as it helps you from being pulled forward. When the natural endpoint is reached at the bottom and you feel a slight stretch in your hips and lower back, drive your hips forward and up for the next repetition.

DOUBLE SWING: KEY POINTS

1. Set up as you would for a double clean.
2. Look straight ahead throughout the movement.
3. Use a strong backswing to start movement.
4. Extend your knees and hips, and swing forward.
5. When the kettlebells reach eye level, allow gravity to bring them down, without letting go.
6. Allow the kettlebells to pass your knees, and spring back up for the next repetition.

Alternating Clean

The alternating clean is an interesting exercise. It is really good for working your grip, forearms, and cardiovascular system. The range of motion is short when compared to the other variations of the clean, so you have to be very explosive with your hips.

Set up as you would for the double clean. You can either stand up with both kettlebells or start with one already cleaned to a racked position. Regardless of how you start, however, at least one kettlebell needs to be lined up with the center of your body. When I teach this exercise, I tell my students to concentrate on cleaning the lower kettlebell. Gravity helps you lower the one on your shoulder.

As you clean the bottom kettlebell, tip the elbow with the racked kettlebell up. This sends it forward and down. When you drive up for the clean portion of this movement, you will most likely extend your ankles as well as your hips and knees. This brings you up on your toes, giving you some extra power to help compensate for the short range of motion. Try to get into a rhythm, and just hop into each repetition.

Alternating Clean   Alternating cleans are a finely choreographed dance. As one bell comes up, the other comes down. Though the range of motion is short, use your legs to hop the weight up as much as possible.

1. Set up as you would for a double clean.
2. Clean one kettlebell to the racked position, and center the other between your knees.
3. Bend your knees and hips, and clean the bottom weight. As it rises, tip your top elbow to lower the top kettlebell. All of this happens at the same time.
4. The alternating clean is performed in a rhythmical hopping motion.

Double Row

The double row is another simple, yet very effective, kettlebell exercise for the upper back. The stabilizing muscles of your trunk are worked as well, as they provide support for your upper body.

Set up as you would for a double clean. Stand up to a fully erect position with both kettlebells. Bend at your waist and knees until your upper body is almost parallel with the ground. Tighten your abdominals and spinal erectors so your trunk is stable. Looking straight ahead, draw your hands to your ribs and pause briefly. Slowly lower the kettlebells until your arms are in a fully extended position just inside of your knees.

Note: There are several grip variations for the double row, depending upon what you would like to emphasize. All variations work the upper back; however, you can also target your biceps, rear shoulder, or the outside of the large upper-back musculature. For the biceps, you can use a supine (palms up) grip. For the rear shoulder, a prone (palms down) grip with your elbows flared out is recommended. Last, for the large latissimus dorsi (upper back) muscles, you can use a neutral (palms in) grip and keep your elbows tight to your sides.

Double Row To get low and use the large muscles of the upper back for this exercise, it is very important to sit back into the double row. If you do not, you will find yourself standing more erect with every repetition and using the muscles of the arms almost exclusively. Also, to help you maintain balance, keep your eyes directed either straight ahead or down very slightly—avoid looking straight down.

DOUBLE ROW: KEY POINTS

1. Set up as you would for a double clean.
2. Grip the weights, and stand up to a fully erect position.
3. Slowly bend at the waist and knees until your upper body is almost parallel to the floor.
4. Tighten the muscles of your trunk.
5. Pull your hands to your ribs, and pause briefly.
6. Slowly lower the kettlebells until your arms are fully extended.

One-Stays-Up Press

In this variation of the press, one of the kettlebells is fully extended overhead at all times. You alternate kettlebells but always keep one pressed. This exercise really works the small stabilizing muscles of the rotator cuff as well as the triceps and larger shoulder muscles.

Set up as you would for any double press. Slightly bend your knees, and tighten your abdominal muscles to stabilize

One-Stays-Up Press   The starting point for the one-stays-up press is really when both bells are extended fully overhead. As the name implies, one kettlebell stays extended while the other is lowered to the shoulder and pressed back up. As you fatigue, resist the urge to lower your extended kettlebell. Be conscious of keeping one arm pressed at all times.

your trunk. Take a deep breath, and then press both kettlebells overhead. Keeping one arm extended, bring the other kettlebell down until your elbow is tucked into your side. Press it back up, and pause briefly with both kettlebells fully extended overhead. Continue to alternate sides until your set is complete.

ONE-STAYS-UP PRESS: KEY POINTS

1. Set up as you would for any double press.
2. Slightly bend your knees and tighten your abdomen.
3. Press both kettlebells to full extension.
4. Keeping one arm extended, lower the other kettlebell.
5. Press the kettlebell back up, pause, and then lower the other kettlebell.
6. Continue to alternate until the set is complete.

Double Squat

Clean the kettlebells to a racked position. Spread your feet slightly wider than shoulder width, and turn your toes outward. Pull your shoulders back, and look up slightly. Begin the movement by bending your knees just before you begin to bend your hips. This helps keep you upright. Squat as deeply as you can, preferably until your thighs are just below parallel to the ground. Exhale forcefully, and drive through the floor back up into a standing position. The double squat and its variations are among the best lower-body exercises out there, and they work the thighs and trunk extremely well.

DOUBLE SQUAT VARIATION: FRONT SQUAT

To emphasize the quadriceps muscles of the thighs, bring your forearms together so the kettlebells are in front of your body. This shifts the line of gravity forward and places more weight on the front of your thighs. Prop your heels up on a board or a mat approximately 1 to 2 inches high. Place your feet shoulder-width apart and point them straight ahead. Look up a little more than normal, and squat down as you would for a conventional double squat.

Double Squat   The double squat with kettlebells is not about weight so much as it is about leverage and posture. Keep the kettlebells back if your feet are flat, and high on your chest if your heels are raised. Look straight ahead or up slightly, and squat as low as you are able. The deeper the squat, the more fully you will develop your hips and legs. Avoid rounding your back at any time during this movement.

DOUBLE SQUAT: KEY POINTS

1. Clean the kettlebells into a racked position.
2. Set your feet according to the squat variation you wish to use: feet wider and toes out for hips; feet closer and toes straight for quads.
3. Adjust the position of the kettlebells according to style: out for conventional; together in front for front squat variation.
4. Take a deep breath. Then start the squat by bending your knees slightly, followed by your hips. This should be a smooth transition.
5. Squat as deep as you are able, making it your goal to go just past parallel.
6. Exhale forcefully at the bottom, and explode back up to a standing position.

Single Floor Press

Lay on the floor next to your kettlebell so it lines up with your midsection. Slide your hand through the handle with your palm up. Pull the kettlebell to your chest, and turn your elbow out so your upper arm is at a right angle to your body. Take a deep breath, and then exhale while pressing the kettlebell up and over so it is lined up with the midline of your body. Slowly lower the kettlebell until your elbow gently touches the floor, and pause briefly. Keeping the tension in your chest, shoulder, and triceps, press the weight back up for the next repetition.

SINGLE FLOOR PRESS: VARIATIONS

By varying the position of the active arm you can emphasize different muscle groups. Keeping your elbow close to your body works more triceps, and a wider elbow emphasizes more outer chest. To build in variety, you can switch your grip periodically.

Single Floor Press   Keep your knees bent to relax your lower back and help you balance the asymmetry of one weight. Start with your elbow flared out from your body. As you press the kettlebell, bring it in line with the center of your chest. Do not bring it over too far, however, to avoid dropping the weight. When lowering the bell, allow your elbow to gently touch the floor.

SINGLE FLOOR PRESS: KEY POINTS

1. Lay on the floor next to the kettlebell so it lines up with your abdomen.

2. Slide your hand through the kettlebell with your palm up.

3. Pull the kettlebell to your chest, and turn your elbow out.

4. Take a deep breath, and press the kettlebell up and over the middle of your chest.

5. Slowly lower the weight until your elbow gently touches the floor.

6. Pause briefly, keeping the tension through your chest, shoulder, and triceps.

7. Press back up.

A QUICK CHANGE IN DIRECTION

Week 5 of this program will make you feel as if your spouse has asked you to pass a few standard sobriety tests after you've been out all night with your friends. The kettlebell lunges, both forward and backward, and kettlebell passes will make you feel like you have never truly learned how to walk, but the strength and balance you develop will be well worth it. Add to this the weight and position of the kettlebells, and your lungs will be on fire as well as your muscles. With all of these exercises, take care to not allow your knee to move past the toes of your front foot. Otherwise, this creates a shearing force that your patellar tendon and your knee will probably not like.

The figure 8 is a movement fairly unique to kettlebell training. It is similar to dribbling a basketball over and over between your legs. You want to use your whole body and sway from side to side as well as forward and backward slightly. It teaches you to stay low for an extended period of time, which is valuable in many sports. It also teaches you how to move your hips from side to side. Both of these things work the muscles of the thighs and trunk well. I recommend that this exercise be performed with a moderate weight for more repetitions. This exercise works best in a lighter range than cleans, for example.

The squat-press is the cousin to the squat-pull. Body position is essentially the same, except that the weight is on the chest for the squat-press and is pressed overhead instead of pulled to the chest. This is a great movement for a football lineman or any athlete who needs to push from the ground up through the hands. The squat-press is sometimes used with the squat-pull as a stand-alone workout because almost all of the major muscle groups of the body are worked between these two exercises.

Last, you will perform the double floor press. This exercise is very similar to the dumbbell press, although the range of motion is somewhat shortened because this is performed from the floor. Your elbows stop just short of a complete range. This works well for athletes who have minor shoulder injuries. Also, the forearms and pectorals are required to be active throughout the movement to keep the kettlebells from falling outward, since they sit to the sides of the forearms instead of lining up directly with them.

Kettlebell Back Lunge

For the kettlebell back lunge, you can use either one or two kettlebells. They can be cleaned to a racked position, they can be at your sides, or a single kettlebell can be resting on your chest. Looking straight ahead, step back slightly farther than you would for a normal stride. Your front foot should remain flat, and your back foot should be on its toes. Bend your back knee first to keep your body upright, and drop as close as you can to the floor without touching. Both your back and front knees should be at right angles. Bring the back leg forward to the starting position, and then step back with the opposite leg. Continue to alternate until your set is complete.

Kettlebell Lunge Whether you are lunging forward or backward, it is very important to work in right angles. Both knees should be bent to 90 degrees at the midpoint of any lunge. Failure to adhere to this rule will result in an irritation of your patellar tendons and soreness in your knees. The easiest way to keep your knees working at this angle is to take a moderate to large stride and to bend your back knee slightly before your front knee regardless of the direction of the lunge. Also, note that the model is looking straight ahead. Doing this helps you keep from leaning forward.

KETTLEBELL BACK LUNGE: KEY POINTS

1. Decide on using one or two kettlebells and whether they will be at your chest, shoulders, or sides.

2. Look straight ahead, and step back with one leg.

3. Keep your front foot flat and your back foot on its toes.

4. Bend your back knee first, and drop down as close as you can to the floor without touching. Both knees should be bent to right angles.

5. Step forward with your back leg, and step back with the opposite leg.

6. Continue to alternate legs until the set is complete.

Caution: To avoid unnecessary stress on your knees, your front knee should not move beyond the toes of the same leg.

KETTLEBELL FORWARD LUNGE

Like the kettlebell back lunge, the kettlebell forward lunge can be performed with one or two kettlebells and held either at the chest, shoulders, or sides. You use the same series of movements as for the kettlebell back lunge, except you step forward. All lunges can be performed while either stationary or walking. I do, however, recommend avoiding backward walking lunges unless you have excellent balance and have experience with this exercise.

Kettlebell Pass

The kettlebell pass is similar to a kettlebell forward lunge, although it is always performed with one kettlebell. Start the movement with the side that is not holding a kettlebell. As you step forward and your front knee bends, pass the kettlebell under your knee to your free hand. Then step with the other side, and pass it back. Continue to alternate sides in this fashion. Look straight ahead or slightly down as you perform this exercise. Also, try to keep a fairly straight back. This exercise works the muscles of the legs, shoulders, and back. It is especially good for developing coordination for sports that require you to move with and around an object, such as wrestling, judo, and jujitsu.

KETTLEBELL PASS VARIATION

This exercise can be performed forward, backward, and diagonally. Experiment with different combinations of directions such as two steps backward followed by one step forward, diagonally in each direction. Repeat this drill several times to get used to changing directions.

Kettlebell Pass   Think of the kettlebell pass as a lunge variation with a shortened range of motion. Your knees do not bend nearly as much as in a traditional lunge, but you still bend forward to coordinate the kettlebell passing behind your knee. This exercise is all about timing. As your knee bends, the kettlebell should be moving behind it. As you take your next step, the kettlebell should be coming up to prepare for the next pass.

KETTLEBELL PASS: KEY POINTS

1. Begin by holding one kettlebell at your side.
2. Step forward with your free side.
3. Keeping your back flat, bend your front leg.
4. Pass the kettlebell underneath your front knee to your free hand.
5. Pass the kettlebell back and forth underneath your front knee as you step.

Figure 8

The figure 8 is a fun exercise that is good for developing strength in your trunk and hips. Just as it sounds, the kettlebell moves around your legs in a figure 8 pattern. Begin by positioning your feet slightly wider than your shoulders. Using a moderate weight, begin with a backswing between your knees. Instead of bringing the kettlebell forward, move your hips to one side and pass the kettlebell behind that knee. As your free hand

Figure 8   Bring the kettlebell straight back between the knees when performing the figure 8. Then take it to the outside and behind the knee for the pass. This gives you a little extra room to keep from banging the kettlebell into your shin. Also, your hips should be moving side to side with the kettlebell. This helps bend your knee and make a gap for the kettlebell to move through.

takes the weight, bring the kettlebell around the outside of your leg and then back between your knees. As the kettlebell passes between your knees, lean to the opposite side and pass the kettlebell behind that knee. Continue to move the kettlebell in a figure 8 pattern until your set is complete. As you perform this exercise, look down at an angle of approximately 45 degrees and keep your back flat. Also, squat down slightly throughout the movement. This exercise is to be performed for a fairly high number of repetitions—usually 20 or more.

FIGURE 8: KEY POINTS

1. Stand with your legs slightly wider than shoulder-width apart.
2. Begin movement with a backswing.
3. Shift your hips to one side, and pass the kettlebell behind that knee.
4. Circle your leg to the front; then pass between your knees.
5. Hand off to your free hand behind the opposite knee.
6. Continue to move in a figure 8 pattern.

Caution: Make sure you have trimmed nails, as they might get caught when changing hands with the weight.

Squat-Press

This exercise can be performed with either one or two kettlebells. If using two, clean them to your shoulders. If using one, rest the kettlebell on your chest with the handle facing your body. Make sure to wrap your thumbs around the handle to secure the weight.

Looking straight ahead, bend your knees as far as you are able (your goal should be to get your thighs parallel to the ground), and then extend your knees and hips. When you reach a fully erect position, continue the movement by pressing the kettlebell(s) overhead. Pause briefly, and then lower the kettlebell(s) to your starting position. As soon as the weight makes contact with your body, drop down into the next repetition.

Squat-Press The key point to remember about the squat-press is that both the downward and upward phases should be performed smoothly. The entire movement from the bottom of the squat to the full extension of the press should be executed in one nonstop motion. The same is true for going back down, from the top of the press to the bottom of the squat. Also, as with most overhead exercises, press the kettlebells to full extension without allowing them to drift forward at the top.

SQUAT-PRESS: KEY POINTS

1. Position yourself with either one kettlebell on your chest or one on each shoulder in a racked position.
2. Look straight ahead, bend your knees, and then bend your hips, dropping into a deep squat.
3. Press your feet into the floor, and explode out of the bottom position.
4. When you are standing erect, follow through into the press.
5. Pause and then lower the kettlebell(s) to the starting position.
6. As soon as the weight makes contact with your body, drop into the next repetition.

Double Floor Press

Set two kettlebells on the floor slightly wider than shoulder-width apart. Lay down between the kettlebells so they are lined up with your midsection. Slide your hands through the handles with your palms up, and pull the weights to your chest. As with the single floor press, turn your elbows out so your arms are perpendicular to your body. Keeping your knees bent and your feet flat on the floor, press both kettlebells to a full extension and center them over your chest. Pause briefly, and then slowly lower the weights until your elbows gently touch the floor. Keeping the muscles of the chest, shoulders, and triceps tight, pause briefly once again and then press the kettlebells back up for the next repetition.

Caution: If you are exercising on a hard surface, use a mat or some towels to cushion the floor.

Double Floor Press   The double floor press calls for two kettlebells to be pressed at the same time. Balance is challenged less in the double press versus the single press; however, you now have the ability to add a significant amount of weight and give your upper body a great workout. As you press, remember to center the kettlebells at the top to maximize the range of motion.

DOUBLE FLOOR PRESS: KEY POINTS

1. Set two kettlebells on the floor slightly wider than shoulder-width apart.
2. Lay between the weights so the handles line up with your midsection.
3. Slide your hands through the handles, palms up.
4. Pull the kettlebells to your chest, and turn your elbows out.
5. Press to full extension over the center of your chest.
6. Pause at the top, and then lower slowly until your elbows lightly touch the floor.
7. Pause at the bottom while keeping tension in your chest, shoulders, and triceps.
8. Press into the next repetition.

COMBINATIONS

A DROPKICK TO YOUR WHOLE SYSTEM

Week 6 consists of three huge combination movements: the double clean-squat, the double clean-squat-press, and the kettlebell push-up–row. Each of these is tough enough to be a stand-alone workout for an unconditioned athlete. Fortunately, you have been training for the last five weeks and are prepared for this. The chapter begins with the double clean-squat. This movement combines the power development of the double clean with the basic strength and leg development of the double squat. Each repetition consists of a clean and a squat. So yes, you have to clean the kettlebells every time. Be sure to keep your head up throughout this exercise. Poor posture becomes exacerbated as fatigue sets in, making it more difficult to complete each repetition. Conversely, an upright posture allows you to maximize your technique.

Upon the completion of the double clean-squat, your lower back will be fatigued but you will probably still have some energy left in your legs and definitely in your shoulders. This is a good time to start the double clean-squat-press. As you descend to the bottom position, think of yourself as a spring that is compressing. When you reach at least 90 degrees, explode upward and follow through into the press. The transition should be very smooth and powerful. You pause briefly when your arms are fully extended, to retain control, and then lower the kettlebells to your shoulders. Tip your elbows up to direct the kettlebells forward, and then explode back into your next clean. You will perform a clean, squat, and press with every repetition. This is a great exercise for any athlete who needs to jump or combine lower- and upper-body power, such as football and volleyball players.

The kettlebell push-up–row is the last exercise in this series. It is a brutal upper-body movement, but it gives your legs and lower back a needed break. You alternate between working your upper back and your chest. Take special care in selecting the kettlebells you use. It is necessary to have kettlebells with a base wide enough so they do not tip over when you are performing push-ups—usually weights of 50 pounds or greater. Ideally the kettlebells will be of the same weight. If they are not, just switch them after a set number of repetitions so that each side receives the same amount of work. You begin by placing your hands inside the kettlebells to perform your push-ups. I have found that the risk is not worth the reward when it comes to performing push-ups from the handles of the kettlebells. It is very likely that you will injure yourself when doing this—for little or no gain. Push-ups from the insides of the handles work just as well.

After you have performed your preset number of repetitions, remove one hand from inside the handle and grip the top of the same handle. Stabilizing with your weightless hand, row the kettlebell to your body. My preference for this exercise is to alternate between one row, one push-up, and then one row on the opposite side. I would count this group of movements as one repetition. When performed in this fashion, kettlebell push-up–rows challenge your cardiovascular system as well as your musculoskeletal system.

There are two other ways to perform the kettlebell push-up–row when the bases of your kettlebells are too small or you have only one kettlebell. The first is to keep one hand on the floor or on a block. You could work one side until that part of the set is finished or you could get up and switch sides every repetition or two. For example, one hand is inside the handle and you perform a push-up; then remove the hand and perform a row. Then get up, switch sides, and repeat. The other method of performing kettlebell push-up–rows is to perform all of your push-ups on the floor. You would be giving up a small portion of the range of motion but not so much as to lessen the value of this exercise. Simply row one kettlebell, remove your hand, perform a push-up, and then slide the kettlebell to the other side and perform a row. Any of these methods will work well so long as you give your full effort.

Double Clean-Squat

The double clean-squat combines two big movements. With all of the muscle that is put into play, your heart, legs, and back get a great workout. Each repetition consists of a full double clean and a full squat.

Set up as you usually would for a double clean. Keeping your head up, clean both kettlebells and pause briefly. Then bend your knees and hips, and squat as deeply as you are able (to spice up your workout, you can add a pause at the bottom of the squat). Extend your knees and hips, and stand up to a fully erect position. Tip your elbows up to direct the kettlebells forward. Then swing the kettlebells between your knees to begin the backswing for the next clean.

Double Clean-Squat   Begin the double clean-squat in exactly the same way as you would the double clean. Once the kettlebells are shouldered, bend your knees and then your hips, and drop into the squat. The more your skill develops with this exercise, the faster you will be able to transition from the clean to the squat and back up again.

DOUBLE CLEAN-SQUAT: KEY POINTS

1. Set up for a double clean.
2. Clean both kettlebells to the racked position, and pause briefly.
3. Bend your knees and hips, and squat down to at least 90 degrees if able.
4. Explode out of the bottom position, and stand up straight.
5. Tip your elbows up to direct the kettlebells forward.
6. Allow the kettlebells to swing between your knees for a backswing.
7. Clean the kettlebells back up for the next repetition.

Double Clean-Squat-Press

Perform the double clean-squat portion of this exercise the same as before. But instead of tipping the kettlebells forward after your rise out of the squat, follow through into the press. You want to use the momentum generated by your legs as you explode out of the bottom position and punch the kettlebells to a full extension overhead. After you fully extend your arms, pause briefly for control, and then lower the kettlebells back to your shoulders. Tip the kettles forward for the next

Double Clean-Squat-Press   Work this exercise in the same way as the double clean-squat. The addition of the press adds extra range of motion and therefore more work. Practice your transitions with this, and all, combination movements.

clean. This is a great exercise for the whole body, and almost no muscle group is spared. It also winds you quickly and can be used as a conditioning exercise as well. Just increase your repetition scheme to a higher range for more of a cardiovascular workout.

DOUBLE CLEAN-SQUAT-PRESS: KEY POINTS

1. Clean both kettlebells at the same time.
2. Pause briefly, and then squat as deeply as you are able.
3. Explode out of the bottom position to a fully erect stance.
4. The moment your knees are straight, punch the kettlebells overhead.
5. Pause briefly, and then lower the kettlebells to your shoulders.
6. Tip the kettlebells forward, and allow them to swing between your knees for the next clean.

Kettlebell Push-Up-Row

Place two kettlebells of sufficient size on the floor, slightly wider than shoulder-width apart. Line the handles up in a straight line. Slide your hands through the handles with your palms down, and get into a push-up position. Execute a push-up as deeply as you are able. When your arms are fully extended, take one hand off of the bell and grip the handle. Row the kettlebell to your body until your hand touches your ribs. Lower the kettlebell, and then slide your hand back inside the handle. Execute another push-up; then proceed to row the opposite kettlebell. Continue to alternate rows on each side while performing a push-up between each one. This exercise works the chest, shoulders, triceps, biceps, and upper back, as well as the stabilizing muscles of the trunk.

Safety Note: You definitely want to use kettlebells with a wide base so that the weights do not tip over during this exercise. You can also use a modified version that involves performing the push-up off of the floor. One kettlebell would then be rowed while the other hand stayed on the floor. The push-up portion of this exercise can be performed from your knees or your toes depending upon your level of strength.

KETTLEBELL PUSH-UP-ROW: KEY POINTS

1. Place two kettlebells on the floor slightly wider than shoulder-width apart with the handles in a straight line.

2. Place your hands inside the handles with your palms down.

3. Perform a push-up; then remove one hand and grip the kettlebell handle.

4. Row the weight to your midsection, and then place the kettlebell back on the floor.

5. Put your hand back inside the handle, and perform another push-up.

6. Repeat the row on the opposite side; then perform another push-up.

7. Continue to alternate rows on each side, performing a push-up between each row.

Kettlebell Push-Up–Row   Note that the model's hand moves from inside of the handle for the push-up to outside of the handle for the row. Push-ups, as a general rule, should not be performed on top of the handles, because of the risk of tipping the kettlebells over.

BIG AND BALANCED

Week 7 will test even the most well-conditioned athlete. It includes a list of combination exercises where each component is a brutal stand-alone exercise. It begins with the double snatch–overhead squat. After you snatch two kettlebells overhead with as much force as you can muster, you must then squat down to below 90 degrees while holding both kettlebells at full extension. This exercise has a very high impact on all systems involved and is extremely challenging to your balance, especially in the bottom position.

As if the double snatch–overhead squat isn't difficult enough, the level of difficulty can be increased with the addition of a press. For this variation, after you have completed the overhead squat, you proceed into a double overhead press that starts in the extended position. The bells are then lowered to the shoulders and pressed, then lowered again to the shoulders, and then lowered between the knees. This completes one full repetition.

You then move on to the one-stays-up row. This exercise involves two kettlebells and is similar to the one-stays-up press regarding the lack of complete rest during the set. One kettlebell stays pulled to your midsection, while the other is rowed. I recommend alternating kettlebells at this point, although you can work one side completely and then the other if you wish. I find it interesting that this exercise is just as tough on the thighs, hips, and low back as it is on the muscles of the arms and upper back, because you will use them as stabilizers throughout your set.

And finally, the alternating press-up into an arms-extended crunch is one of my favorite floor exercises. It works the anterior deltoid and the triceps without a doubt. The neat thing, however, is that you are crunching up on one side as you press. This works the pectoral muscles very deeply and lets you bring your abdominal muscles into play as well. The press-up is great for striking and blocking sports such as boxing or karate. When your set of press-ups is complete, you hold both arms at full extension and continue the set by crunching straight up. This is difficult in terms of muscular endurance for both the abdominal muscles as well as the triceps and deltoids, which are now acting as stabilizers. All in all, this is a fun exercise.

Double Snatch– Overhead Squat

Begin by setting up two kettlebells of moderate weight for a double snatch. Snatch the kettlebells, and look up slightly. Turn your toes out slightly as well. Keeping your abdominal muscles tight, squat as low as you are able. It is critical that you keep your back flat and your shoulders pulled back as well as your head up. Explode out of the bottom of the squat; then lower the kettlebells to your shoulders. Tip your elbows up to direct the kettlebells forward and into a backswing. Snatch both kettlebells again for your next repetition.

Double Snatch–Overhead Squat   This exercise is arguably one of the most difficult in all of kettlebell training. You absolutely must keep your head up and arms extended if you are to maintain your balance. Practice getting into a deeper squat each time you perform this exercise.

DOUBLE SNATCH–OVERHEAD SQUAT: KEY POINTS

1. Set up two kettlebells of moderate weight for the double snatch.
2. Snatch both kettlebells overhead.
3. Turn your toes out slightly, and keep your head up.
4. Squat as deep as you are able with your arms extended overhead.
5. Explode out of the bottom of the squat.
6. Lower the kettlebells to your shoulders; then tip the kettlebells forward to go into the next repetition.

Note: It helps to wear footwear with a little bit of a heel such as a hiking boot or work boot if you don't have weightlifting shoes. Sneakers will do as well if that is all that you have available. Also, anyone with shoulder issues should not attempt this exercise.

DOUBLE SNATCH–OVERHEAD SQUAT VARIATION: DOUBLE SNATCH–OVERHEAD SQUAT–PRESS

This overhead squat variation combines three big movements into one. The important thing to remember is to break it up into its component lifts until you feel comfortable with it. This is the big brother to the double snatch–overhead squat. You perform this exercise in exactly the same way except that you insert a press into the very top of the movement. Same rules apply: keep your head up and back straight.

Set up as you did for the double snatch. Snatch the kettlebells overhead; then drop into your squat. Drive out of the bottom position, keeping your arms extended overhead. When you are standing fully erect, lower the kettlebells to your shoulders, and then press them back up. This is one repetition. Once again lower the kettlebells to your shoulders; then tip them forward to begin your next repetition.

DOUBLE SNATCH–OVERHEAD SQUAT–PRESS: KEY POINTS

1. Set up for a double snatch.
2. Snatch both kettlebells.
3. Keeping your arms extended overhead, squat as low as you are able.
4. Explode out of the bottom position.
5. Lower the kettlebells to your shoulders.
6. Press the kettlebells back up to full extension.
7. Again, lower the kettlebells to your shoulders, and tip them forward to begin the next repetition.

One-Stays-Up Row

The one-stays-up row is a great exercise for the upper back. Line up two kettlebells as you would for any double row. Pull both kettlebells to your ribs. Then, keeping your shoulders level, lower one until your arm is completely extended. Row the kettlebell back up and pause briefly with both elbows tucked into your sides; then lower the opposite kettlebell. Continue to alternate kettlebells until your set is complete.

One-Stays-Up Row   The key point to this exercise is to maintain correct posture so that the upper back is performing the majority of the work. Stay low and sit back. Only one arm is rowing at a time. The other stays up.

ONE-STAYS-UP ROW: KEY POINTS

1. Line up two kettlebells just inside your feet as you would for any double row.
2. Select the grip that most suits your needs.
3. Bend at your waist and knees as you normally would for a double row.
4. Pull both kettlebells to your midsection.
5. Lower one kettlebell until your arm is fully extended.
6. Pull it back up to your midsection.
7. Pause briefly, and then lower the opposite kettlebell.
8. Continue to alternate kettlebells until your set is complete.

Note: This exercise can be performed using a variety of grips, depending upon what movement or muscle group you want to emphasize. Palms up (supine) adds resistance to the biceps. Palms facing each other (neutral) helps you focus more on the large latissimus dorsi muscles of the upper back. Palms down (prone) with your elbows flared out emphasizes the back of your shoulders and middle of your upper back. You could also use a rotating grip by starting with your palms in a prone position and rotate them up into a supine position at the top of the row.

Alternating Press-Up (from Floor)

The difference between a floor press and a press-up is that when performing press-ups, you are actually crunching up at the top of the movement and your upper body is rising off of the floor.

To perform this movement, set up as you would for a floor press. Be sure you are on a padded surface. Begin pressing one kettlebell to full extension so it is lined up with the middle of your chest. Brace your free arm against the floor, and as the kettlebell is being pressed, rise off of the floor into a diagonal crunch. You will rise up onto the elbow of your free arm. Slowly lower your back, shoulders, and head; then bend your elbow until it gently touches the floor. Repeat the press and crunch with the opposite side. Continue to alternate sides until your set is complete.

ALTERNATING PRESS-UP (FROM FLOOR): KEY POINTS

1. Set up for a double floor press.
2. Begin pressing one kettlebell to full extension so it is lined up with the middle of your chest.
3. As the kettlebell is being pressed, brace your free arm against the floor.
4. Using your abdominal muscles, crunch into the press, raising your back, shoulders, and head off of the floor.
5. Slowly lower your upper body to the floor; then lower the kettlebell until your elbow gently touches the floor as well.
6. Repeat the movement on the opposite side.
7. Continue to alternate until your set is complete.

Alternating Press-Up (from Floor) This is very similar to both the single and double floor presses. The biggest difference is the addition of a crunch at the top of each press. Follow through with the press, and lift the weighted shoulder off of the floor. Use your lower elbow to brace off of the floor.

TOTALLY TWISTED TRAINING

If you thought Week 5 tested your balance with lunges, passes, and figure 8s, I've got news for you: it was only warm-up for Week 8. The program for Week 8 first loosens you up with a one-hand swing refresher; then it moves on to side bends, get-ups, stand-ups, and a double snatch refresher; and it finishes with the one-stays-up floor press into leg raise. The one-hand swing is included because it is one of the most fundamental kettlebell movements and should be practiced from time to time by even the most experienced kettlebell practitioners.

You then are twisted and turned like a pretzel with side bends. Some kettlebellers call these windmills. They are very similar to the triangle pose in yoga, with the difference being the kettlebell in your top hand. This movement is great for flexibility as well as strength for the abdominal and lower back muscles. It takes a bit of practice to understand positioning, so start light and stick with it.

The next exercise on the list is the get-up. It is, quite simply, moving from a supine position on the floor to standing completely upright. It involves an entire series of movements that are to be performed while holding a kettlebell fully extended over your head. It takes quite a lot of balance and concentration. When it is performed with moderate to heavy weight or for a high number of repetitions, your cardiovascular system kicks into high gear to get blood to all of the muscles being used. It is definitely a great exercise for whole-body strength and good for any martial arts or grappling sport.

Stand-ups are very simple yet very effective leg movements. You usually want to hold the kettlebells at your chest or shoulders, although taller people can get away with keeping them at their sides. You want to keep your toes curled under your feet. These are what are known as live toes. They help you push off of the floor. Also, when performing stand-ups, your moving leg actually sweeps around as it comes up. This is extremely beneficial not only for developing strength in your thighs but also for getting used to changing your body positioning back and forth between high and low. Stand-ups are great for anyone who needs to get off the ground quickly or needs to be able to adjust his or her height. A great example of this would be a wrestler moving in for a single-leg takedown.

The double snatch is such a huge kettlebell movement that I thought it would be fitting to bring it up once again. Remember that it is just like the single snatch, save for the addition of lowering the kettlebells to your shoulders before lowering them to the knees. This will keep you from being pulled forward by the large amount of weight. The double snatch involves a great deal of muscle mass and a big range of motion, so be prepared for a high-heart-rate, high-impact exercise.

The one-stays-up floor press finishes out the exercise list for Week 8. It is great for working your chest, shoulders, and triceps and has the added benefit of making your shoulders pull double duty as both prime movers and stabilizers. When the presses are completed, you move into leg raises while keeping your arms extended. The extended arms not only add to the difficulty of the exercise but also help hold your torso still while you work your abdominal muscles. This position is actually quite comfortable and generally feels better than most other methods of performing leg raises.

One-Hand Swing (Refresher)

As the name states, this movement is very similar to the two-hand swing. There are some subtle differences, however. Set

One-Hand Swing (Refresher)   It is definitely worthwhile to go back to some of the basic ballistic kettlebell movements. The one-hand swing is a movement that doesn't go out of style and should be reintroduced to your routine periodically. Remember, the positioning for the one-hand swing is the same as for the two-hand swing, with two exceptions. First and most obvious, the grip is with one hand instead of two. Second, to center the kettlebell between the knees, you have to lean slightly away from it. The swing pattern still needs to follow the midline of the body, whether you are using one hand or two.

up the same way you would for a two-hand swing regarding posture and foot placement. When you grip the handle, however, make sure to center the kettlebell between your knees. Start with the same backswing as you would for the two-hand swing; then drive the kettlebell forward and up with your hips and thighs. Gently follow through with your shoulder until the kettlebell reaches eye level. Remember to continue to center the kettlebell throughout the movement.

ONE-HAND SWING: KEY POINTS

1. Set up as you would for a two-hand swing.
2. Keep the kettlebell centered.
3. Drive from your hips, thighs, and lower back.
4. Follow through with your shoulder until the kettlebell is eye level.
5. Let gravity pull the kettlebell down for the next repetition.

Side Bend

This exercise is great for developing strength, flexibility, and balance in your midsection. Snatch or clean and press a kettlebell overhead. Take a wide stance. Turn out the foot of your free side so it is perpendicular to the foot of your weighted side. Lower your free hand to the inside of your thigh on your free side, and turn your palm up. Look up at the kettlebell, and then very slowly start to lean to your free side. Bend the knee of your free side as well; then begin to lean forward slightly. Your goal is to eventually be able to slide your free hand to the inside of your foot. When you have stretched as far as you are able, straighten back up to your starting position. Perform just a handful of repetitions before you switch to the other side. This exercise takes great concentration and needs to be performed very slowly. Repetition ranges of 3 to 5 per set work well.

Side Bend   When performing the side bend, the kettlebell should always be lined up with the center of your base of support. This is the point directly between your feet. Also, to help you keep this proper body alignment, your eyes should never leave the kettlebell. Remember to relax your hips and lean forward slightly when bending over.

SIDE BEND: KEY POINTS

1. Snatch or clean and press the kettlebell overhead.

2. Take a wide stance.

3. Turn out your free foot until it is perpendicular to your opposite foot.

4. Place your free hand inside of your free thigh with your palm up.

5. Look up at the kettlebell, and then very slowly start to lean away from the weight.

6. Bend the knee of your free side slightly, and then begin to lean forward while continuing to look at the kettlebell.

7. Slide your free hand as low as you are able.

8. Slowly straighten back up for the next repetition.

Get-Up The get-up has many steps, but it is not as complicated as it looks. The important things to remember are to always keep your eyes on the kettlebell and to take your time until you get the hang of it. Break it up into steps.

Get-Up

Lay on the floor as you would for a single floor press. Press the kettlebell in one hand to full extension. Keeping your eyes on the kettlebell, shift your hips to your weighted side so you are lying on your free side. While continuing to look at the kettlebell, crunch up using your abdominals, and then use your free hand to assist you to a kneeling position. Using your weighted foot, step up so your foot is flat and press it into the floor until you are in a standing position. You should be using the toes of the opposite foot for assistance when you are starting to stand. At this point you should be standing fully erect and looking up at your kettlebell. Your weighted arm should be completely locked out.

Now you want to reverse the entire series of movements. Very slowly, kneel down on your free leg; then lower your weighted leg until you are kneeling down on both knees. Place your free hand on the floor behind you, and lower yourself to your free hip. Using primarily your abdominal muscles, lower your upper body the rest of the way to the floor, and then lower the kettlebell to your starting position. Do all of these movements while continuing to look at the kettlebell for posture and stability.

Like the side bend, this exercise is to be performed very slowly and for a limited number of repetitions per set. Try performing 3 to 5; then switch sides or alternate for a total of 10.

GET-UP: KEY POINTS

1. Set up as you would for a single floor press.
2. Press the kettlebell to full extension.
3. Looking at the kettlebell, shift your hips to the weighted side so you are lying on your free side.
4. Using your abdominal muscles, crunch halfway to a sitting position.

5. Use your free hand to assist in raising your body into the kneeling position.
6. Step up with your weighted foot so it is flat.
7. Pushing off of your weighted foot and toes of your free foot, press into the floor until you are in standing position.
8. Reverse this series of movements. Begin by stepping back with your free foot until you are kneeling on that side.
9. Step back with your weighted foot until you are on both knees.
10. Place your free hand on the floor behind you.
11. Lean back on your free hip.
12. Use your abdominal muscles to slowly lower your upper body to the floor.
13. Finish by lowering the kettlebell to the starting position.

Stand-Up (from Knees)

Begin by kneeling down on both knees with two kettlebells in the racked position. Step up with one foot so it is flat. The toes of your other foot should be curled underneath. Push off of your flat foot as well as the toes of your back foot, and stand up so your feet are even. Step back with your lead foot, and return to a kneeling position. Step back up with the other foot, exchanging lead feet. Again, lead with that foot to a kneeling position. Continue alternating lead feet until your set is finished.

STAND-UP (FROM KNEES): KEY POINTS

1. Clean two kettlebells into the racked position, and kneel down on both knees.
2. Begin the first repetition by stepping back up with one foot, then the other.
3. Step back down to a kneeling position with the same lead leg.
4. Change lead legs, and step up with the other leg. Continue to alternate.

Stand-Up (from Knees) Stand-ups from your knees require you to keep your abdominal muscles tight and your lower back straight. As you fatigue, the tendency is to lean forward to compensate for tired thighs. Focus on keeping your trunk straight to keep the tension on your thighs and off of your knees.

Note: This exercise may be performed either by leading with one side for a specified number of repetitions and then the other, or by alternating feet every full repetition. Also, because you are on your knees, you may want to use some sort of padding for comfort.

Double Snatch (Refresher)

The double snatch is performed with two kettlebells. Set up as you would for a double clean. Keeping your head up and your shoulders back, take a big backswing. Explode forcefully from the bottom, and drive with your whole body. When the kettlebells are approximately 12 inches from the top position, push into the handles as you would for a single snatch. When this is executed properly, there is very little impact on the forearms. At this point, lower the kettlebells to your shoulders, and then tip your elbows to direct the kettlebells downward. This step keeps you from being moved off-balance by the weights. Swing the kettlebell between your knees, and explode back up for the next repetition.

Double Snatch   The flat back and correct posture in the beginning of the double snatch make all the difference in the success of this movement. Note that at midpoint, the knees and hips are extended to transfer the momentum gained in the bottom position to the lockout. At the endpoint of the movement, the weights are fully extended overhead and are properly aligned with the body's base of support.

DOUBLE SNATCH: KEY POINTS

1. Set up as you would for the double clean.

2. Use a strong backswing.

3. Snatch both kettlebells as you would for a single snatch.

4. Push into the kettlebells 12 inches before the top of the movement.

5. Lower the kettlebells to your shoulders before tipping down into the next repetition.

One-Stays-Up Floor Press (into Leg Raise)

In this variation of the press, one of the kettlebells is fully extended over your chest at all times. You alternate kettlebells but are always keeping one pressed. This exercise really works the small stabilizing muscles of the rotator cuff as well as the chest, triceps, and larger muscles of the shoulders.

Set up as you would for a double floor press. Take a deep breath, and then press both kettlebells over your chest. Keeping one arm extended, bring the other kettlebell down until your elbow lightly touches the floor. Press it back up, and pause briefly with both kettlebells fully extended. Continue to alternate sides until your set of presses is complete. While continuing to hold both kettlebells at full extension, you then raise both legs straight up to begin performing your leg raises. Keeping both legs together and straight, lower them approximately halfway to the floor. Contract your abdominal muscles and rotate your hips back. Pull your legs up past your waist until they are over your chest. Your hips should actually rise off of the floor slightly.

ONE-STAYS-UP FLOOR PRESS: VARIATIONS

The one-stays-up floor press can be varied by changing up the follow-up exercises. For example, instead of leg raises after the press, you can perform trunk twists or leg sweeps while holding the kettlebells.

One-Stays-Up Floor Press (into Leg Raise)   The one-stays-up floor press (into leg raise) is fairly straightforward. The main point to remember is that when you are finished with your presses, keep the kettlebells fully extended and balanced while you perform the leg raises.

ONE-STAYS-UP FLOOR PRESS
(INTO LEG RAISE): KEY POINTS

1. Set up as you would for a double floor press.
2. Press both kettlebells to full extension.
3. Keeping one arm extended, lower the other kettlebell.
4. Press the kettlebell back up, pause, and then lower the other kettlebell.
5. Continue to alternate until the set is complete.
6. Continue holding both kettlebells at full extension.
7. Put your legs together, and raise them straight up.
8. Lower your legs halfway to the floor.
9. Pull them back over your chest, raising your hips off of the floor slightly.

MORE KETTLEBELL MOVEMENTS

By this time you have finished the eight-week program, you have an introductory knowledge of kettlebell training, and your body has been conditioned. This chapter discusses more kettlebell movements that you might want to try at some point in the future. I have selected a few of my favorites, but still many more are out there waiting to be tried.

This section begins with walking swings, which help get you used to moving with weight. They continue in the tradition of other swing variations by helping you move with the momentum of the bells and not fight it. This is a great movement for any sport where you are in contact with a moving object or an opponent, such as field events or grappling sports.

Next is the kettlebell crawl. This exercise is just plain brutal. It hammers your upper body and forces it to grow stronger. You work the muscles of your upper back, biceps, and shoulders very intensely, as well as your chest and triceps for support. Like the name implies, it involves getting onto all fours and moving two kettlebells forward for distance. Ideally, you would stand on your toes and drag your legs while performing this exercise.

Even if you have to use some leg strength, it is still an overall great upper-body movement.

When it comes to developing crushing grip strength, something often overlooked in sports training, the bottoms-up press works wonders. The bottoms-up press is less about the press than it is about the bottoms-up. To perform this exercise, you hold a kettlebell upside down and press it to full extension. To keep the kettlebell from tipping over, you are forced to squeeze the handle as hard as you can. Trust me when I say that this is no easy feat. A very strong athlete can bottoms-up press upward of 65 pounds. I have even seen feats that involved weights well over 100 pounds. No matter the weight you start with, however, the important thing is to progress slowly and steadily. When you get stuck on a weight, you can add to its difficulty by off-centering the weight slightly. This forces you to grip it even harder to maintain control. When you have mastered that weight at all angles, you can then give the next weight up another shot.

One of my all-time favorite trunk-strengthening exercises is the next exercise on this list: the overhead towel swing. It is very similar to swinging Scottish- or Olympic-style hammers. Lace a sturdy towel, rope, or belt through the handle of the kettlebell. Take care in selecting your weight. Too light, and you will have the kettlebell moving at speeds you might not be able to control. Too heavy, and you will fail to swing it around your head and may hit yourself along the way. For most men, I like to start at 35 pounds. I will start most women with somewhere around 20 to 25 pounds. Every athlete is different, so feel free to experiment in a very open, safe environment. When performing the overhead towel swing, you should rely on the strength of your midsection and not your arms. This exercise is devoted to building your core—no beach muscles allowed.

In the last part of this section I included the pullover, the triceps extension, and the hammer curl. Though I do not feel that these are among the most important kettlebell exercises, I do think they are fun and give you a physical and psychological break. I call these exercises dessert work. You get your main nutrients from snatches and cleans, and then you can finish off your kettlebell meal with some extensions and curls.

Walking Swing

This exercise is great for getting the feel of the kettlebell, as well as for conditioning. Make sure you have plenty of room for this exercise. Set up as you would for a single swing, the two-hand swing, or a double swing. You swing the kettlebell(s) as you would for any swing variation, but you also take one step with each foot as a follow-through. Step forward with the momentum of the kettlebell.

Walking Swing Make sure you have plenty of room when performing walking swings. Also, look straight ahead to help you keep your balance. Move with the weight, and do not fight it.

WALKING SWING: KEY POINTS

1. Set up for any style of swing.

2. Proceed with the swinging movement.

3. When the kettlebell reaches eye level, take one step forward with each foot.

4. Allow the kettlebell to swing down between your knees and then back up for the next swing-step combination.

Kettlebell Crawl

Line up two kettlebells shoulder-width apart. Grip the handles, and step back so your body is as close to parallel with the ground as your strength allows. You should look as though you are getting into a push-up position. Spread your feet so they are slightly wider than shoulder-width. Pull one kettlebell off of the floor, and move it forward approximately 12 inches. As the kettlebell moves forward, step forward with the leg on the same side. Repeat these movements with the opposite side. Continue to alternate sides until you have achieved your goal.

Kettlebell Crawl When crawling with the kettlebells, keep as much of your body weight on your feet as is necessary. Be careful not to lean too far forward and tip over the bells.

1. Make sure you have adequate space for this exercise, as well as appropriately sized kettlebells.
2. Set up two kettlebells shoulder-width apart.
3. Gripping the handles, get into a push-up position with a wide stance.
4. Lift one kettlebell, and move it forward approximately 12 inches.
5. As you move the kettlebell, move the leg on the same side forward the same distance.
6. Repeat on the opposite side, and continue to alternate.

Note: This exercise is not for beginners. To avoid injury, be sure to use kettlebells with a sufficiently wide base—usually 50 pounds or greater. Narrow kettlebells are likely to tip over and injure your wrist. Also, be aware of how much weight you place on your hands. This may need to be adjusted as you fatigue.

Bottoms-Up Press

This exercise is awesome for developing crushing grip strength as well as stability in the muscles of your trunk. You can grip the kettlebell anywhere on the handle you wish as long as the kettlebell is upside down.

Set up as you would for a single or double press. Grip the handle(s) as tightly as you can, and clean the kettlebell(s) into the rack position. Slowly press the kettlebell(s) to full extension, and very slowly lower the kettlebell(s) back to your shoulder(s). Continue until you have reached your goal.

Bottoms-Up Press Begin by crushing the handle of the kettlebell with your hand. Curl or clean it to your shoulder, and then press it overhead. Be sure to keep your hand and forearm directly beneath the center of the handle to keep it from tipping over. If you want to make this exercise more difficult, intentionally grip the kettlebell off-center. This forces you to use even more grip strength to keep the bell from tipping over.

BOTTOMS-UP PRESS: KEY POINTS

1. Use a moderate weight.
2. Set up as you would for a single or double press.
3. Grip handle(s) as tightly as possible.
4. Clean kettlebell(s) to the rack position.
5. Maintaining your balance, slowly press the kettlebell(s) to full extension.
6. Slowly lower the kettlebell(s) to your shoulder(s), and repeat the series of movements until your set is finished.

Overhead Towel Swing

This is a great exercise for the trunk muscles. It is similar to the hammer swing in track and field or the Highland games. Start with a moderate weight, and make sure you have plenty of room. Lace a thick towel or rope through the kettlebell handle. Grip the towel so the kettlebell is approximately 2 to 3 feet from your hands. Plant your feet slightly wider than your shoulders, and hold firmly onto your towel. Create a neutral line of sight by picking something straight ahead to focus on; this will help you to maintain your balance. Start by slowly swinging the kettlebell side to side like a pendulum. When the kettlebell

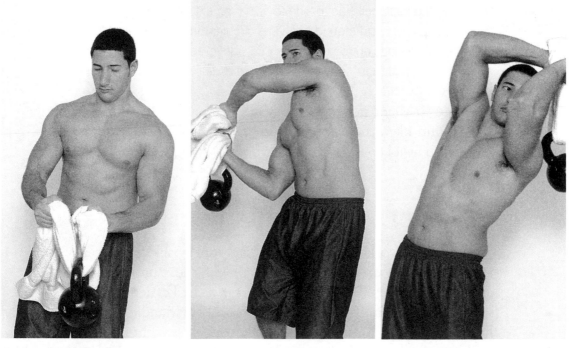

Overhead Towel Swing   With overhead towel swings, always make sure you have ample space. Keep your eyes directed straight ahead to help you maintain balance. As you swing the kettlebell around your body, lean back and rotate your trunk. Strength for the towel swing comes from your abdominal muscles and lower back, not your arms.

gains sufficient momentum, rotate both hands over and around your head. Gradually pick up speed without losing control. Pull the kettlebell around your body in a circular motion, using the muscles of your trunk. When you have completed your repetition goal for one direction, slow the kettlebell down until it gradually comes to a complete stop. Then repeat the exercise on the other side.

OVERHEAD TOWEL SWING: KEY POINTS

1. Run a thick towel through the handle of a kettlebell of moderate weight.
2. Take a firm grip on each end so the kettlebell is about 3 feet from your hands.
3. Swing the kettlebell side to side to gain momentum.
4. Pull hands over and around head in a circular motion.
5. When repetitions are complete on one side, gradually slow to a complete stop, and then repeat on the opposite side.

Note: It is not necessary to swing the kettlebell parallel to the ground like a helicopter blade. It only needs to move fast enough to avoid contact with your body.

Pullover

This exercise works the muscles of the upper back and triceps as well as those around your chest and ribs. Lie on the floor, and pull a kettlebell onto your chest. Grip the kettlebell on its sides so your thumbs are wrapped around the handle and the handle is facing your chin. Press the kettlebell straight up; then begin the pullover by lowering the kettlebell over your head to the floor while keeping your arms straight. Inhale deeply as you lower the kettlebell; then exhale forcefully as you pull it back over your chest.

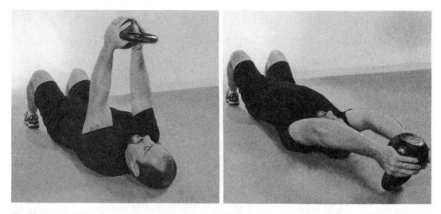

Pullover   Keep your knees bent and feet flat on the floor when performing pullovers. Try to inhale deeply as you lower the kettlebell to the floor. Then exhale forcefully as you pull the kettlebell over your chest. Make sure you have a tight grip on the weight, with your fingers wrapped around the handle.

PULLOVER: KEY POINTS

1. Lie on the floor with the kettlebell on your chest.
2. Grip the kettlebell's sides so your thumbs are wrapped around the handle and your palms are wrapped around the ball. The handle should face your chin.
3. Press the kettlebell straight up; then lower it over your head to the floor while keeping your arms straight.
4. Pull the kettlebell back over until it is over your chest.

Triceps Extension

This exercise obviously works the triceps and can be performed standing, sitting, or lying down. Hold the kettlebell on the sides so your thumbs are wrapped around the handle and the handle is facing your chin, just like for the pullover. Press your arms to full extension, bend your knees slighty, and then lower the kettlebell back behind your head if you are standing or sitting.

Your arms should be bent to at least 90 degrees before being brought back to the starting position. If you are lying on the floor or on a bench, you can lower the kettlebell above your head or to the side, alternating after each repetition. When you have reached the bottom of the movement, extend your arms so they are completely straight at the top.

Triceps Extension (Standing) Keep your knees bent slightly throughout the triceps extension to keep you from leaning backward as you fatigue. Looking straight ahead, extend the weight completely overhead.

Triceps Extension (Lying)   Lower the kettlebell to the side of your head (alternating sides) or over your head. Then extend your arms straight.

TRICEPS EXTENSION: KEY POINTS

1. Select a position: standing, sitting, or lying.

2. Hold the kettlebell on its sides with your thumbs wrapped around the handle.

3. Press to a full extension; then lower according to your body position.

4. Bend your elbows at least 90 degrees; then extend back to the starting position.

Hammer Curl

This exercise works the biceps as well as the muscles of the forearms. It can be performed by holding the sides of the kettlebell or kettlebell handle or by holding a towel that is running through the kettlebell.

Grip the kettlebell or towel firmly; then bend your knees slightly. Pin your arms to your sides and bend your elbows so your hands come up to your chest. Slowly lower the kettlebell until your hands are below your waist and in the starting position.

HAMMER CURL: KEY POINTS

1. Grip the kettlebell or towel firmly.
2. Keep your back straight and your knees slightly bent.
3. Pin your arms to your sides, and bend your elbows until your hands reach your chest.
4. Slowly lower the kettlebell until your hands are in the starting position.

Hammer Curl   Keeping your knees bent, bend your elbows and bring the kettlebell to your chest. To gain the most benefit from this exercise, tuck your elbows into the side of your body to keep from cheating.

GOAL SETTING
THE BIRTH OF THE BABY

10

As I have written previously, when I first started with kettle-bells most of the ones I came across were too light to meet my needs. Eventually I had a friend at a local foundry make some for me. After he made the first few kettlebells, I decided I wanted something that looked like one an old-time strong-man would use. I didn't realize that in those days kettlebells were hollow so you could adjust the weight by adding or removing metal shot. I found a medicine ball, which was slightly bigger than a basketball, and brought it to my friend. I told him I would like him to make me a kettlebell using the medicine ball as a size reference. With one eye arched and a smirk on his face, he agreed.

About a week later he called me up and said it was finished, and for some reason he began to laugh. Not understanding what was funny, I called my friend and judo instructor, Tom, and said, "It's ready." Before I could get another word out, he said he would pick me up. What seemed like a minute later, he pulled up in his truck and told me to get in. He then proceeded to make any NASCAR fan proud and drove as fast as he possibly could without actually running over any smaller vehicles. When we arrived at the foundry, the guys in the shop were all smiling. What was there was the biggest kettlebell I had ever seen. It was also the heaviest. It weighed 145 pounds. My friend Tom said, "That thing is the size of a baby." It was actually more like a toddler. The heaviest kettlebell I had worked with up to that point was 66 pounds.

"What are you gonna do with it?" one old-timer snickered.

"Lift it, of course," I said.

When he walked away, I turned to Tom and said, "How *are* we going to lift this thing?"

We took the kettlebell back to my gym and just stared at it. It must have been funny, in an odd way, to see two grown men staring in complete silence for several long minutes at a ball made of iron. Finally I said, "We need to get stronger."

This was actually an epiphany for me. At that moment, after all of my years of training, I finally realized that we are bound only by the limitations that we impose upon ourselves. Only we ourselves can decide what we can and cannot accomplish. I devised a program based upon what I could do with it. I could perform limited-range, two-hand swings and squat-pulls. Over the next few months, these movements led to one-hand high pulls to my chin and assisted (with the opposite hand helping) single cleans. Finally the day arrived when I gripped it and yanked it to my shoulder.

I have since lifted more weight with one hand for cleans, presses, and other movements, but that first clean with the Baby was probably the one I'm most proud of. It was the first time I ever took something I thought was impossible and turned it into a challenge.

The point of this story is that we all need to set goals. Training aimlessly is the same as driving aimlessly. You will not end up where you want to be. My advice is to set small goals that are very achievable and to build your confidence. Even if your long-range goals seem unattainable at first, you may very well achieve them over time. Let's be realistic, some goals may never be attained. But I argue that you are still better off for having tried. One thing is for certain, though: forgotten dreams will absolutely never become reality.

Can an Athlete Ever Be Too Strong? . . . Maybe!

If you ask any strength-training enthusiast, myself included, whether an athlete can ever be too strong, the answer that instantly comes to mind is, "Absolutely not!" When you reflect upon this answer, however, it must be answered again with, "Maybe." Strength is only one attribute that makes up an athlete. Different sports require different amounts of strength. They also require different types of strength. Building maximum strength, for example, might not be the most practical approach when repetitive strength endurance is called for. Yes, an increase in maximum strength will increase strength endurance, but focusing most of the training efforts on strength endurance will produce better results for that particular athlete.

If your sport demands a high degree of speed and your conditioning is aimed at something else, you have to reevaluate the design of your training program. Most sports require a mixture of strength, speed, agility, power, flexibility, endurance, and so on. Also, each athlete is unique. Athletes vary in genetic potential, motor skills, age, sex, height, weight, psychological makeup, and so on. This is where the art of program design comes into play. These are all things with a scientific basis, but in the end it takes the ability to think abstractly to view the sum of all of these attributes. The program needs to be flexible because life is unpredictable. One athlete might have the flu, and another may not cope with stress adequately. Active and nonactive rest must be employed whenever necessary. So to answer the question, "Can an athlete be too strong?" the answer is no, as long as the athlete is not gaining strength to the detriment of some other quality he or she needs for optimal performance. Remember, most sports are a mixture of attributes. The training program must address the conditioning of all these qualities in the proper ratio so the athlete performs optimally.

Progressing with Kettlebells

There are many ways to progress with a resistance training program. Designing a training program around a long-term goal and then breaking it up into shorter-term goals produces the best results. You are, however, dedicating the program to a specific goal, and it will be slightly more difficult to switch directions if your goals change in the middle of the program.

Another option is to train with a more general, nonspecific program that is flexible. For example, you might work in a moderate range for both volume and intensity with basic exercises such as cleans and snatches, and then use a short (three- to six-week) peaking period when a specific task arises. Whatever path you choose will produce results, but it is up to you to decide which will meet your needs. Again, your body will adapt specifically to what you do to it. There are two basic conditions to this statement:

1. You must give your system enough training stimulation to cause it stress. Here, stress is a good thing. Without stress, there is no need for adaptation, but in this case, adaptation is the training effect you seek.
2. You must allow your system to recover and adapt. If you overwhelm your body and mind by not getting enough rest or by exceeding your ability to tolerate volume and intensity, you will not be able to adapt to your training stress.

Let us examine the variables of training again to explore how we might adapt to different types of stress and therefore make progress. This section will specifically examine volume, intensity, and density. Most major sports, however, require a specific ratio of these variables as well as many others, so it is not necessarily easy to isolate them and then design a program.

Increase one, and you might lose the ability to recover from another. It can be a very delicate balance.

VOLUME

Volume can be defined as your total workload. To increase volume, you simply must do more work. One way to add extra work is to perform more repetitions per set. However, if you are already training at your repetition maximum, this obviously will not work. At this point you must add more sets, more exercises, or more training sessions. Adding more sets is fairly easy to do, but remember the basic conditions for adaptation. More is not necessarily better. When you add more sets, you must be conscious of your total workload. Adding a set to an exercise will not add greatly to your training stress. Adding a set to every exercise in a program, however, may increase your total workload greatly.

You may also increase your workload by adding more exercises. This can be done per training session, weekly, monthly, or by phase. For example, you may be working with ten exercises on Monday, eleven on Wednesday, and twelve on Friday. You might also try ten exercises Week 1, eleven in Week 2, and twelve in Week 3. Last, you can increase your training load by adding work sessions. You can do this by adding training days: increasing from three days per week to four, for example.

You might also train more than once in the same day. Most athletes think of strength training once per day, three or four times per week. Many advanced kettlebell practitioners, however, have been able to achieve amazing results by slowly building their tolerance to volume over time. They might train with many short sessions in one day on most days. This allows them to work with a total volume many times that which you would normally see recommended in a magazine or book. In strength circles, Eastern Europeans are known for this type of training. Again, it takes time and consistency to achieve this.

I recommend starting slow with two to three sessions per week. Start with a handful of basic exercises; then add a few more over time. At this point, start adding sets and repetitions. When you feel that you have done all you can with three sessions, try four, and so on.

Listen to your body, and build in lots of rest and active rest. Not every training session has to be your best ever for it to help you produce a training effect. We are looking for long-term results gained slowly and permanently. Your training is like an investment. If you add to it over time and are patient, it will grow. If you check it daily and agonize over it, you will probably not last very long.

INTENSITY

Intensity is how much work you pack into a particular set or repetition. A clean performed with a 95-pound kettlebell is more intense than a clean performed with a 50-pound kettlebell. The 95 obviously weighs more than the 50.

You can also view intensity by comparing one exercise to another in terms of complexity and range of motion. A bicep curl performed with 50 pounds is not as intense as a snatch performed with 50 pounds. More work was performed during the snatch because of a much greater range of motion. Keep this in mind when you are designing your program, because you cannot value all exercises equally in terms of stress on your system. A training program, with many single-joint exercises, is less stressful and requires less recovery time than a program that is heavy with deadlifts, squats, cleans, and snatches.

When increasing intensity, progress slowly and methodically just as you would add volume. Small increases in weight and exercise complexity work well. I try to limit my increases in weight to between 1 and 2 percent per week. Less-experienced lifters might be able to go as high as 5 to 10 percent when they are beginning. Over time, these small increases really add up.

Things slow down quite a lot over time, but progress can still be made. I usually increase intensity for a few weeks and then have to back off significantly—by at least 10 to 20 percent. I will then start back up with a weight I find moderately challenging and work from there.

DENSITY

Last, density can be defined as how much work is performed in a given time period. For example, performing 100 repetitions of kettlebell snatches with a 50-pound bell in 10 minutes is denser than performing the same work in 20 minutes.

Density is often overlooked when a person is designing programs. It is actually quite valuable in terms of athletics because so many sports have a time component. Basketball has periods, boxing has rounds, and football has quarters, to name a few. Sports can break down even further in density. Most major sports are intermittent and have an average interval of play. Kettlebell training can be progressed not only by adding sets and repetitions, but also by decreasing rest periods so that play, combat, or whatever the task can be more closely mimicked. This will better prepare the athlete for the real thing.

I have used the manipulation of density to produce great results with certain types of athletes. Wrestlers, depending upon their specific brand—that is, folk style, free style, Greco-Roman—do quite well with density training. High-school wrestlers use three 2-minute periods. Ultimately their strength and conditioning should reflect this. As the wrestlers go through their competitive season, they should be tapering their conditioning down to three very intense 2-minute periods. This can be adapted to tournament situations as well. If athletes expect to compete in many tournaments, they can structure their kettlebell training the same way. They could use three 2-minute periods followed by a 5- to 10-minute break, and repeat this scenario five times to simulate five matches. It is better to prepare for the worst than hope for the best.

To increase your training density, you can gradually reduce the rest periods between repetitions, sets, and exercise cycles. Here is an example of a program for a mixed martial artist training for a single match. Unless he or she is fighting for a championship, this athlete will most likely be fighting three 5-minute rounds. I would start the athlete out with a high volume to develop a solid foundation. It would include a lot of cardiovascular training. Over the course of the program, I would reduce the volume in favor of a higher intensity until ultimately the athlete is training for three to five periods of 3 to 5 minutes in duration with 1-minute rest breaks. I would make these as intense as the athlete could tolerate.

Putting It All Together: Basic Program Design

As with other training programs, kettlebell programs require you to address variables such as intensity, density, and volume. They differ from typical fitness programs, however, because they are not organized in a bodybuilding fashion. For example, Day 1 in a weekly training cycle may focus on a large pull like a clean, instead of attempting to isolate a muscle group like the biceps. The purpose of this book is to teach you how to enhance your sport, not necessarily to develop larger arms. In this instance, and with all sport training programs, function leads form, not vice versa. Focus on the attributes of your sport, and you will take on the look of that type of training. Trying to look like a bodybuilder will enhance your sport only if you are a bodybuilder; otherwise it will enhance your sport performance very little.

Remember, if you start with the basic premise that your body will respond specifically to what you do to it, then it is really very simple to design an effective program. Whether you want to train for muscular endurance, hypertrophy, power, maximum strength, or a combination of these, success lies in simplicity. In other words, design your program the very way you want to perform. Lift heavy weights if that is your goal. Be explosive if it is power you want. Train with high volume if it is fatigue you wish to overcome.

The simplest way to organize a kettlebell regimen for a sport is to determine your needs and then start with the basics. Ask yourself how your sporting season is scheduled throughout the year. In your off-season, you should be able to afford time to train with a greater volume and have more time for recovery. During the preseason, you want to perform your most serious preparatory work and increase the intensity on the large-volume foundation you have already built. During the in-season, common sense tells us to cut back on the volume but to remain in competitive form with brief, intense training sessions. Last, the postseason is a time to step back and take some complete rest and then gradually work back into some low-intensity, low-volume work.

Since all sports are different in their scheduling, for the sake of simplicity we will estimate each season to be three months in duration. If your sporting seasons are set up differently, simply adjust them accordingly. If you participate in more than one sport, use the training for the first sport as your preparatory period for the second. If your sports do not run in succession, use a brief off-season period before beginning the preseason training for your next sport.

OFF-SEASON

Start with the off-season training period. You can estimate this to be approximately six months away from your competitive season and to last for three months. The main focus of this phase is to work on general conditioning and on increasing your overall work capacity. At this point, do not worry about sport specificity. Maintain the general skills necessary for your sport—

such as running, jumping, throwing, kicking—but spend the majority of your time working on basic strength, flexibility, and cardiovascular conditioning.

When learning how to use kettlebells, start with a few low-repetition sets of a handful of different exercises. For example, one to three sets of 3 to 5 repetitions of five to ten different exercises. This workout should be performed three days per week. Add one repetition per workout per exercise. At the end of the month, add one or two exercises to the program and switch around the order of exercises for variety. Your weights should gradually increase, but an increase in intensity should be secondary to an increase in volume. Your off-season program might look like as follows:

OFF-SEASON
Weeks 1–4

Three times per week

Two-hand swing
One-hand swing
Single snatch
Single press
Bent-over row
Squat-pull
Sidewinder
Single clean
Double floor press into leg raise (arms extended)
Alternating press-up

- *Perform one set of each exercise for 5 repetitions.*
- *Add 1 repetition to each set with each workout.*
- *Drop the repetitions back to 5 per set in Week 4.*
- *Rest up to 3 minutes between exercises throughout the four-week period.*

Weeks 5–8

Three times per week

Single snatch
Double snatch
Single clean
Double clean
Alternating clean
Double press
One-stays-up row
Squat-pull
Double floor press
Alternating press-up
Get-up

- *Perform one set each for 5 repetitions.*
- *Add 1 repetition to each set with each workout.*
- *Drop the repetitions back to 5 per set in Week 8.*
- *Shorten the rest period to no more than 2 minutes between exercises.*
- *Work through the list of exercises twice, top to bottom.*

Weeks 9–12

Three times per week

Double clean
Squat-pull
Double snatch
Squat-press
One-stays-up press
One-stays-up row
Sidewinder
Kettlebell push-up–row
Kettlebell crawl
Alternating press-up
Alternating press-up into leg raise
    (arms extended)

- *Perform one set each for 5 repetitions.*
- *Add 1 repetition to each set with each workout.*
- *Drop the repetitions back to 5 per set in Week 12.*
- *Shorten the rest period to no more than 1 minute between exercises.*
- *Work through the list of exercises three times, top to bottom.*

Again, this is only a sample program. Personal training programs vary greatly depending upon the needs of the athlete. As you can see, the volume was gradually increased over the twelve-week period as was the complexity of the exercises. Also, the volume was decreased significantly every fourth week to allow the athlete to recover before the next phase of increased volume and complexity. I've experimented with these active rest periods in the past and have found them to work best every three to five weeks, with the average being every fourth week. If volume and intensity are especially high, you will need "light weeks" more frequently. Lower-volume, lower-intensity training necessitates less frequent "light weeks."

PRESEASON

The preseason is the time to really turn up your training. This is when you use the foundation of higher volume you built in the off-season to push your limits. Both volume and intensity are increased during this phase. This phase is extremely stressful both physically and psychologically and necessitates more frequent light weeks to aid in recovery. You also want to step up your specific skill training as well. Soccer players, basketball players, and baseball players should be kicking, throwing, passing, shooting, or whatever it is they do in season—just in a slightly less organized format than that of the regular season. Also, athletes should be participating in light competition if their sport allows, such as pickup games and friendly scrimmages.

Assume you are approximately three months away from the competitive season. This phase will be very taxing, so you need to make a special effort to warm up and stretch before your workouts and to get plenty of sleep. Your kettlebell program might now look as follows:

PRESEASON

Weeks 1–3

Three times per week

One-hand swing
Single snatch
Double snatch
Double clean
Alternating clean
One-stays-up press
One-stays-up row
Squat-pull
Alternating press-up into leg raise
    (arms extended)

- *Perform one set each for 5 repetitions.*
- *Add 1 repetition to each set with each workout.*
- *Drop the repetitions back to 5 per set in Week 3.*
- *Do not rest between exercises.*
- *Work through the list of exercises four times, top to bottom.*
- *Rest 3 minutes between each cycle.*

Weeks 4–6

Three times per week

Figure 8
Squat-pull
Side shuffle
Squat-press
Sidewinder
Kettlebell forward lunge
Kettlebell pass
Single clean
Single snatch
Single floor press

- *Perform one set each for 5 repetitions.*
- *Add 1 repetition to each set with each workout.*
- *Drop the repetitions back to 5 per set in Week 6.*
- *Do not rest between exercises.*
- *Work through the list of exercises five times, top to bottom.*
- *Rest 3 minutes between each cycle.*

Weeks 7–9

Three times per week

One-hand swing
Double swing
Single clean
Side bend
One-stays-up press
Squat-pull
Sidewinder
Overhead towel swing
Get-up
Kettlebell crawl

- *Perform one set each for 5 repetitions.*
- *Add 1 repetition to each set with each workout.*
- *Drop the repetitions back to 5 per set in Week 9.*
- *Do not rest between exercises.*
- *Work through the list of exercises six times, top to bottom.*
- *Rest 3 minutes between each cycle.*

Weeks 10–12

Three times per week

Figure 8
Kettlebell pass
Double clean-squat-press
Squat-pull
Side shuffle
Double snatch
Alternating clean
Bent-over row
Double snatch–overhead squat
Alternating press-up

- *Perform one set each for 5 repetitions.*
- *Add 1 repetition to each set with each workout.*
- *Drop the repetitions back to 5 per set in Week 12.*
- *Do not rest between exercises.*
- *Work through the list of exercises seven times, top to bottom.*
- *Rest 3 minutes between each cycle.*

IN-SEASON

The time has finally come for all of your hard work to pay off. You definitely want to continue training with your kettlebells, but your sport must take priority. Kettlebells, at this point, are meant to enhance your athletic performance. You want to decrease the overall volume of training significantly. You may continue to train three days per week or even decrease to two. Also, you want to shorten the length of each workout both in time and in exercise selection. This is to allow proper recovery from the stresses of training and competition. You also, however, want to maintain a rather high degree of intensity so the training effect you have worked for does not diminish. If your program is designed properly, you may even see an increase in the training effect throughout the competitive season. This would be the result of all of the training of the previous months coming into full effect. Your twelve-week in-season phase program might look as follows:

IN-SEASON

Weeks 1–4

Two or three times per week

Two-hand swing
One-hand swing
Single snatch
Squat-pull
Single clean
Double press
Double row
Alternating press-up
Get-up

- *Perform one set each for 5 repetitions.*
- *Add 1 repetition to each set with each workout.*
- *Drop the repetitions back to 5 per set in Week 4.*
- *Do not rest between exercises.*
- *Work through the list of exercises two times, top to bottom.*
- *Rest 1 to 3 minutes between each cycle.*

Weeks 5–8

Two or three times per week

Single snatch
Squat-pull
Single clean
Double press
Double row
Alternating press-up
Get-up

- *Perform one set each for 5 repetitions.*
- *Increase the weight with each set and each workout as you are able.*
- *Drop the weight back by 10 percent in Week 8.*
- *Do not rest between exercises.*
- *Work through the list of exercises two times, top to bottom.*
- *Rest 1 to 3 minutes between each cycle.*

Weeks 9–12

Two or three times per week

Double snatch
Side shuffle
Double clean-squat
Alternating press-up

- *Perform one set each for 5 repetitions.*
- *Increase the weight with each set and each workout as you are able.*
- *Drop the weight back by 10 percent in Week 12.*
- *Do not rest between exercises.*
- *Work through the list of exercises three times, top to bottom.*
- *Rest 3 to 5 minutes between each cycle.*

POSTSEASON

The postseason should be very simple. You should build in as much rest as possible. This does not mean, however, that you will be completely inactive. On the contrary, you should, in fact, be quite busy. Every part of the training year is very important and has its own role to play in your overall program. The focus of your postseason program should be recovery, both inactive and active, as well as preparation for the generalized training of the off-season. Recovery should be both physiological as well as psychological.

Fun should be a major part of this phase. Activities such as swimming, walking, and hiking could be included. Also, strength and flexibility programs such as yoga and Pilates would be appropriate as well. You could take part in sports unrelated to your competitive sport, such as playing basketball for wrestlers or martial arts for football players. All of these things actually aid in recovery as long as they are of a decreased intensity and volume and are not psychologically stressful. Your postseason might look as follows:

POSTSEASON

Week 1

Complete rest

Weeks 2–4

Three times per week

Two-hand swing
Single press
Squat-pull

- *Perform one set each for 10 repetitions.*
- *Increase the weight with each set and each workout as you are able.*
- *Rest 1 to 3 minutes between exercises.*
- *Work through the list of exercises three times, top to bottom.*
- *Rest 3 minutes between each cycle.*

Weeks 5–8

Three times per week

Two-hand swing
Figure 8
Single snatch
One-stays-up press
One-stays-up row
Squat-pull

- *Perform one set each for 12 repetitions.*
- *Increase the weight with each set and each workout as you are able.*
- *Rest 1 to 3 minutes between exercises.*
- *Work through the list of exercises three times, top to bottom.*
- *Rest 3 minutes between each cycle.*

Weeks 9–12

Three times per week

Single snatch
Double clean
Side shuffle
Side bend
Get-up
Single floor press

- *Perform one set each for 15 repetitions.*
- *Increase the weight with each set and each workout as you are able.*
- *Rest 1 to 3 minutes between exercises.*
- *Work through the list of exercises three times, top to bottom.*
- *Rest 3 minutes between each cycle.*

Incorporating Kettlebells into an Existing Training Program

Kettlebells are tools that work great by themselves or can easily be incorporated into an existing program. In fact, a kettlebell might just be the missing piece in your training. For combining power and muscular endurance there is nothing better. This combination of training elements would be appropriate for sports such as soccer, basketball, or any interval sport where conventional bodybuilding movements are not relevant. For grapplers, a heavy kettlebell used for single cleans is about as good as you can get. What else would combine a strong grip and pull on a single side, with a powerful extension of the knees and hips? Here are some examples of how you can use kettlebells in a program with other strength-training implements:

Football Sample Workout

PRESEASON

Weeks 1–3

Monday (Day 1)

Two-hand swing (95 lbs., 10 repetitions)
Dumbbell steep incline press (100 lbs., 10 repetitions)
Double clean (80 lbs., 5 repetitions)
Double clean-squat (80 lbs., 5 repetitions)
Side shuffle (over step) (50 lbs., 10 repetitions)
Tire flip (500–600 lbs., 10 repetitions)

Wednesday (Day 2)

Figure 8 (35 lbs., 20 repetitions)
Side bend (35 lbs., 10 repetitions each side)
Barbell back squat (315 lbs., 10 repetitions)
Double snatch (80 lbs. each, 5 repetitions)
Double clean-press (65 lbs. each, 5 repetitions)
Kettlebell push-up–row (65 lbs. each, 5 repetitions)

Friday (Day 3)

Overhead towel swing (35 lbs., 20 repetitions each side)
Squat-press (80 lbs., 5 repetitions)
Heavy squat-pull (140+ lbs., 10 repetitions)
Sandbag carry (100+ lbs., 10–40 yards)
Weight-sled drag (150+ lbs., 10–40 yards)

- *Add weight, repetitions, or both with each workout, except in light weeks.*
- *Perform each movement powerfully, and be very technique conscious.*
- *Rest 3 minutes between each exercise.*
- *Work through the list of exercises five times, top to bottom.*

As you can see, the kettlebells blend very well with other training tools such dumbbells, barbells, sandbags, sleds, stones, and so on. The weight and repetition schemes would vary throughout this phase as well as throughout the training year, but the kettlebells become part of the regular workout. They are not something to be dusted off every once in a while for the sake of novelty.

Here is another sample program for a wrestler in the preseason. Please note that the only things required are a few kettlebells, a sandbag, and some stones.

Wrestling Sample Workout

PRESEASON

Weeks 1–4

Monday (Day 1)

Single clean (65 lbs., 15 repetitions each side)
Squat-pull (95 lbs., 20 repetitions)
Kettlebell push-up–row (50 lbs., 10 repetitions each side)
Alternating press-up into trunk twist (arms extended) (65 lbs., 10 repetitions each side)

Tuesday (Day 2)

Overhead towel swing (35 lbs., 15 repetitions each side)
Double clean-squat (65 lbs. each, 15 repetitions)
Stone pick-up (to chest) (150 lbs., 10 repetitions)
Stone pick-up (to shoulder) (120 lbs., 10 repetitions)

Thursday (Day 3)

Weighted chin-up (+25 lbs., 10 repetitions)
Kettlebell pass (all directions) (35 lbs., 20 repetitions)
Side shuffle (over step) (35 lbs., 15 repetitions each side)
Sidewinder (95 lbs., 10 repetitions each side)
Sandbag stand-up (from knees) (100 lbs., 5 repetitions each side)

Saturday (Day 4)

Single clean (95 lbs., 10 repetitions each side)
Squat-pull (145 lbs., 10 repetitions)
Alternating clean (65 lbs. each, 5 repetitions each side)
Alternating press-up (65 lbs., 10 repetitions each side)
Get-up (35 lbs., 5 repetitions each side)

- *Add weight, repetitions, or both with each workout, except in light weeks.*
- *Perform each movement powerfully, and be very technique conscious.*
- *Rest 3 minutes between each exercise.*
- *Work through the list of exercises five times, top to bottom.*
- *Reduce the rest breaks 1 minute each week.*
- *Increase rest to 3 minutes and reduce weight by 20 percent in Week 4.*

SAMPLE PROGRAMS FOR
FOOTBALL
AND SOCCER

11

Strength and conditioning for football has changed a lot over the years. When football first came about, athletes did not strength-train at all. Doing so was thought to make the athlete slow and bulky. Then athletes started using barbells and dumbbells in moderation. In the 1970s weight machines came into vogue as high technology, and people thought they produced better results because they were more advanced as well as scientifically studied. Today things are split almost evenly among a high-fatigue circuit called high-intensity training (HIT), Olympic-style lifting that focuses on barbell power cleans, and powerlifting that uses lots of squats and bench presses.

My personal opinion is that all three of these systems have positive and negative aspects. I appreciate the ability to train with the high heart rate gained from HIT. The Olympic lifts offer great development in power and explosiveness. Last, nothing builds overall strength like the heavy squats in powerlifting. The problem is that all of these programs lack what the others have.

The ideal program combines strength, power, and stamina and gives the athlete the ability to demonstrate these attributes repeatedly. To me this seems like a fairly simple training problem to solve. How, you ask? You guessed it, kettlebells! I would also include stones, tires, sleds, and sandbags—things that are free or inexpensive, yet infinitely valuable in developing the perfect football player. The reason these hybrid programs are rare is that people tend to perpetuate the things that they are taught. It is difficult to accept that there are better ways of doing things. I must admit, I was very closed-minded regarding strength training up until I started to seriously work with kettlebells. They made me question everything. My conclusion has been that if someone is getting the results you seek and is using a different methodology, you are obligated as a professional to find out why that person is getting those results.

The following sample program uses just kettlebells. But again, the athlete would greatly benefit from the addition of other training implements.

Football

OFF-SEASON

Weeks 1–4

Three times per week

Two-hand swing
Double press
Double row
Double clean
Kettlebell push-up–row
Squat-pull
Alternating press-up

- *Perform one set each for 5 repetitions.*
- *Add 1 repetition per exercise each workout.*
- *Drop repetitions back to 5 in Week 4.*
- *Rest 3 minutes between exercises.*
- *Work through the list of exercises three times, top to bottom.*
- *Rest 3 minutes between cycles.*

Weeks 5–8

Three times per week

Double clean
Double squat
Double press
Double row
Squat-pull
Side shuffle
Alternating press-up into leg raise
    (arms extended)

- *Perform one set each for 5 repetitions.*
- *Add 1 repetition per exercise each workout.*
- *Drop repetitions back to 5 in Week 8.*
- *Rest 3 minutes between exercises.*
- *Work through the list of exercises four times, top to bottom.*
- *Rest 3 minutes between cycles.*

Weeks 9–12

Three times per week

Alternating press-up into leg raise
    (arms extended)
One-hand swing
Double clean
Double clean-squat
Double clean–squat–press
Side shuffle
Squat-pull

- *Perform one set each for 5 repetitions.*
- *Add 1 repetition per exercise each workout.*
- *Drop repetitions back to 5 in Week 12.*
- *Rest 3 minutes between exercises.*
- *Work through the list of exercises five times, top to bottom.*
- *Rest 3 minutes between cycles.*

PRESEASON

Weeks 1–3

Three times per week

Two-hand swing
Double clean
One-stays-up press
Double clean-squat
Double snatch
Squat-pull
Alternating press-up into leg raise
    (arms extended)

- *Perform one set each for 5 repetitions.*
- *Add 1 repetition per exercise each workout.*
- *Add weight as you are able.*
- *Drop repetitions back to 5 in Week 3.*
- *Rest 2 minutes between exercises.*
- *Work through the list of exercises five times, top to bottom.*
- *Rest 3 minutes between cycles.*

Weeks 4–6

Three times per week

Kettlebell push-up–row
Kettlebell crawl
Single clean
Single press
Side shuffle
Sidewinder
Kettlebell forward lunge
Figure 8
Overhead towel swing

- *Perform one set each for 5 repetitions.*
- *Add 1 repetition per exercise each workout.*
- *Add weight as you are able.*
- *Drop repetitions back to 5 in Week 6.*
- *Rest 2 minutes between exercises.*
- *Work through the list of exercises five times, top to bottom.*
- *Rest 3 minutes between cycles.*

Weeks 7–9

Three times per week

Alternating clean
One-stays-up press
Side shuffle
Double clean
Double squat
Side shuffle
Double clean-squat
Squat-pull
Side shuffle
Kettlebell forward lunge
Alternating press-up

- *Perform one set each for 5 repetitions.*
- *Add 1 repetition per exercise each workout.*
- *Add weight as you are able.*
- *Drop repetitions back to 5 in Week 9.*
- *Rest 2 minutes between exercises.*
- *Work through the list of exercises five times, top to bottom.*
- *Rest 3 minutes between cycles.*

Weeks 10–12

Three times per week

Figure 8
Overhead towel swing
Kettlebell forward lunge
Double clean
Squat-pull
Double snatch
Double clean-squat
Squat-pull
Sidewinder
Side shuffle
Squat-press
Double floor press into leg raise
    (arms extended)

- *Perform one set each for 5 repetitions.*
- *Add 1 repetition per exercise each workout.*
- *Add weight as you are able.*
- *Drop repetitions back to 5 in Week 12.*
- *Rest 2 minutes between exercises.*
- *Work through the list of exercises five times, top to bottom.*
- *Rest 3 minutes between cycles.*

IN-SEASON

Weeks 1–4

Three times per week

Double snatch
Alternating clean
Squat-press
Double clean-squat
Overhead towel swing
Alternating press-up

- *Perform one set each for 5 repetitions.*
- *Add weight as you are able.*
- *Reduce weight by 10 percent in Week 4.*
- *Rest 2 minutes between exercises.*
- *Work through the list of exercises three times, top to bottom.*
- *Rest 5 minutes between cycles.*

Weeks 5–8

Three times per week

Double snatch
Double clean
Double clean-squat
Double clean-squat-press
Side shuffle

- *Perform one set each for 5 repetitions.*
- *Add weight as you are able.*
- *Reduce weight by 10 percent in Week 8.*
- *Rest 2 minutes between exercises.*
- *Work through the list of exercises three times, top to bottom.*
- *Rest 5 minutes between cycles.*

Weeks 9–12

Three times per week

Single clean
Squat-pull
Squat-press

- *Perform one set each for 5 repetitions.*
- *Add weight as you are able.*
- *Reduce weight by 10 percent in Week 12.*
- *Rest 2 minutes between exercises.*
- *Work through the list of exercises three times, top to bottom.*
- *Rest 5 minutes between cycles.*

POSTSEASON

Weeks 1–2

Complete rest

Weeks 3–4

Four times per week

Biking, hiking, running, etc. (20 minutes)
Body-weight abdominal work
Two-hand swing
One-hand swing
Single press
Bent-over row

- *Use light weight.*
- *Perform one set each for 10 repetitions.*
- *Add 1 repetition per exercise each workout.*
- *Rest 3 minutes between exercises.*
- *Work through the list of exercises two times, top to bottom.*
- *Rest 3 minutes between cycles.*

Weeks 5–8

Three times per week

Two-hand swing
One-hand swing
Single clean
Single press
Bent-over row
Side shuffle

- *Use light weight.*
- *Perform one set each for 10 repetitions.*
- *Add 1 repetition per exercise each workout.*
- *Rest 3 minutes between exercises.*
- *Work through the list of exercises three times, top to bottom.*
- *Rest 3 minutes between cycles.*

Weeks 9–12

Three times per week

Body-weight abdominal work
Single snatch
Double clean
Single clean
Alternating clean
Squat-pull
Side shuffle
Kettlebell forward lunge
Single floor press

- *Use light weight.*
- *Increase weight as you are able.*
- *Perform one set each for 10 repetitions.*
- *Add 1 repetition per exercise each workout.*
- *Drop repetitions back to 10 in Week 12.*
- *Rest 3 minutes between exercises.*
- *Work through the list of exercises three times, top to bottom.*
- *Rest 3 minutes between cycles.*

Soccer

OFF-SEASON

Weeks 1–4

Three times per week

Side shuffle
Kettlebell forward lunge
One-hand swing
Single snatch
One-stays-up press
One-stays-up row
Kettlebell push-up–row
Overhead towel swing

- *Perform one set each for 7 repetitions.*
- *Add 1 repetition per exercise each workout.*
- *Drop repetitions back to 7 in Week 4.*
- *Rest 3 minutes between exercises.*
- *Work through the list of exercises three times, top to bottom.*
- *Rest 3 minutes between cycles.*

Weeks 5–8

Three times per week

Side shuffle
Squat-pull
Single snatch
Kettlebell forward lunge
Kettlebell pass
One-stays-up press
One-stays-up row
Overhead towel swing
Alternating press-up into leg raise
    (arms extended)

- *Perform one set each for 10 repetitions.*
- *Add 1 repetition per exercise each workout.*
- *Drop repetitions back to 10 in Week 8.*
- *Rest 3 minutes between exercises.*
- *Work through the list of exercises three times, top to bottom.*
- *Rest 3 minutes between cycles.*

Weeks 9–12

Three times per week

Figure 8
Kettlebell pass
Side shuffle
Squat-pull
Squat-press
Two-hand swing
Double snatch
Double clean-squat
Kettlebell back lunge
Side bend
Overhead towel swing

- *Perform one set each for 10 repetitions.*
- *Add 1 repetition per exercise each workout.*
- *Drop repetitions back to 10 in Week 12.*
- *Rest 3 minutes between exercises.*
- *Work through the list of exercises three times, top to bottom.*
- *Rest 3 minutes between cycles.*

PRESEASON

Weeks 1–3

Three times per week

Two-hand swing
Side shuffle
Kettlebell back lunge
Side shuffle
Double snatch
Kettlebell pass
Overhead towel swing
Kettlebell push-up–row

- *Perform one set each for 10 repetitions.*
- *Add 1 repetition per exercise each workout.*
- *Add weight as you are able.*
- *Reduce weight by 10 percent in Week 3.*
- *Rest 2 minutes between exercises.*
- *Work through the list of exercises four times, top to bottom.*
- *Rest 3 minutes between cycles.*

Weeks 4–6

Three times per week

Single snatch
Double clean
Double clean-squat
Sidewinder
Side shuffle
Figure 8
Kettlebell crawl
Side bend
Get-up

- *Perform one set each for 10 repetitions.*
- *Add 1 repetition per exercise each workout.*
- *Add weight as you are able.*
- *Reduce weight by 10 percent in Week 6.*
- *Rest 2 minutes between exercises.*
- *Work through the list of exercises four times, top to bottom.*
- *Rest 3 minutes between cycles.*

Weeks 7–9

Three times per week

One-hand swing
Single snatch
Single clean
Side shuffle
Kettlebell back lunge
Side shuffle (over step)
Get-up
Kettlebell pass
Kettlebell crawl
Side bend
Pullover
Alternating press-up

- *Perform one set each for 10 repetitions.*
- *Add 1 repetition per exercise each workout.*
- *Add weight as you are able.*
- *Reduce weight by 10 percent in Week 9.*
- *Rest 1 minute between exercises.*
- *Work through the list of exercises four times, top to bottom.*
- *Rest 3 minutes between cycles.*

Weeks 10–12

Three times per week

Figure 8
Overhead towel swing
Kettlebell pass
Kettlebell forward lunge
Side shuffle
Sidewinder
Squat-pull
Kettlebell push-up–row
Side shuffle (over step)
Get-up
Kettlebell pass (all directions)
Side shuffle (over step)

- *Perform one set each for 10 repetitions.*
- *Add 1 repetition per exercise each workout.*
- *Add weight as you are able.*
- *Reduce weight by 20 percent in Week 12.*
- *Rest 1 minute between exercises.*
- *Work through the list of exercises four times, top to bottom.*
- *Rest 3 minutes between cycles.*

IN-SEASON

Weeks 1–3

Two times per week

Double snatch
Side shuffle
Figure 8
Kettlebell back lunge
Kettlebell pass (all directions)
Kettlebell push-up–row
Overhead towel swing
Double floor press into leg raise
    (arms extended)
Pullover

- *Perform one set each for 12 repetitions.*
- *Add 1 repetition per exercise each workout.*
- *Add weight as you are able.*
- *Reduce weight by 20 percent in Week 3.*
- *Do not rest between exercises.*
- *Work through the list of exercises one time, top to bottom.*

Weeks 4–6

Two times per week

Figure 8
Overhead towel swing
Side bend
Single snatch
One-hand swing
Side shuffle (over step)
Stand-up (from knees)
Get-up
Alternating press-up into leg raise
    (arms extended)
Pullover into leg raise (arms extended)

- *Perform one set each for 12 repetitions.*
- *Add 1 repetition per exercise each workout.*
- *Add weight as you are able.*
- *Reduce weight by 20 percent in Week 6.*
- *Do not rest between exercises.*
- *Work through the list of exercises one time, top to bottom.*

Weeks 7–9

Two times per week

Overhead towel swing
Two-hand swing
Double snatch
Alternating clean
Kettlebell forward lunge
Kettlebell back lunge
Kettlebell pass (backward only)
Side shuffle (over step)

- *Perform one set each for 12 repetitions.*
- *Add 1 repetition per exercise each workout.*
- *Add weight as you are able.*
- *Reduce weight by 20 percent in Week 9.*
- *Do not rest between exercises.*
- *Work through the list of exercises one time, top to bottom.*

Weeks 10–12

Two times per week

Kettlebell pass (all directions)
Kettlebell forward lunge
Side shuffle (over step)
Double squat
Side shuffle
Kettlebell crawl
One-hand swing
Overhead towel swing
Alternating press-up
Pullover into leg raise (arms extended)

- *Perform one set each for 12 repetitions.*
- *Add 1 repetition per exercise each workout.*
- *Add weight as you are able.*
- *Reduce weight by 20 percent in Week 12.*
- *Do not rest between exercises.*
- *Work through the list of exercises one time, top to bottom.*

POSTSEASON

Week 1

Complete rest

Week 2

Four times this week

Walking, light jogging, stretching, active rest, etc.

Weeks 3–4

Three times per week

Light jogging, easy interval runs, stretching
Overhead towel swing
Squat-pull
Figure 8
Single press
Bent-over row

- *Perform one set each for 5 repetitions.*
- *Add 1 repetition per exercise each workout.*
- *Add weight as you are able.*
- *Rest 1 to 3 minutes between exercises.*
- *Work through the list of exercises one time, top to bottom.*

Weeks 5–8

Three times per week

Figure 8
Overhead towel swing
Side shuffle
Two-hand swing
Sidewinder
Double press
Double row

- *Perform one set each for 7 repetitions.*
- *Add 1 repetition per exercise each workout.*
- *Add weight as you are able.*
- *Reduce weight by 10 percent in Week 8.*
- *Rest 1 to 3 minutes between exercises.*
- *Work through the list of exercises one time, top to bottom.*

Weeks 9–12

Three times per week

Kettlebell pass (all directions)
Side shuffle
Kettlebell forward lunge
Kettlebell push-up–row
Single snatch
Single clean
Pullover into leg raise (arms extended)

- *Perform one set each for 10 repetitions.*
- *Add 1 repetition per exercise each workout.*
- *Add weight as you are able.*
- *Reduce weight by 10 percent in Week 12.*
- *Rest 1 to 3 minutes between exercises.*
- *Work through the list of exercises one time, top to bottom.*

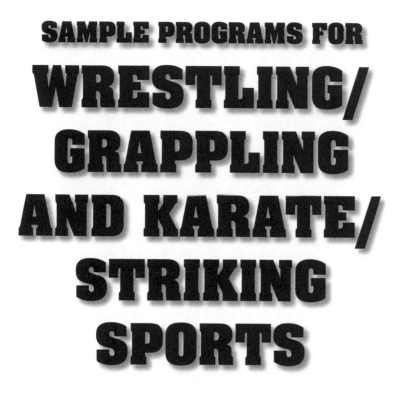

SAMPLE PROGRAMS FOR WRESTLING/ GRAPPLING AND KARATE/ STRIKING SPORTS

12

As mentioned earlier, I initially began training with kettlebells to assist my early-midlife-crisis sport of competitive judo about ten years ago. I was competing against some athletes much younger than me with twenty years of experience. My training partner, Todd, started around the same time that I did. I knew Todd from my days working for a local gym. He was very strong. Todd had shoulders like cannonballs and arms like a gorilla. He was also about a decade older than me. I mention this not to be ageist but simply to paint a full picture. As athletes age, sports requiring stamina become a little tougher to participate in. Also, older athletes are less flexible and heal much more slowly than when they were younger. That being said, Todd and I trained very hard under two very seasoned instructors.

Not long after we began training together, Todd decided to compete in a promotion tournament, which is a contest where the winner stays on the mat to fight. I was nursing a minor shoulder injury and was unable to participate. In this type of contest, if you keep winning, you get to keep fighting. Someone who shows exceptional skill and courage might be promoted in belt rank. The coaches get together at the end of the tournament and discuss whether they felt anyone stood out. Promotion in this fashion is somewhat rare, however.

A black belt from the Ukraine happened to show up. He was of average build and height, but his knowledge and experience far exceeded anyone else's at the tournament. One after another, he easily defeated every competitor who faced him, regardless of the competitor's size or strength. There was not a close match in the group. Then came Todd's turn. He and I had trained hard, but we knew Todd was no match technically for the Ukrainian. He was many belt levels more advanced than Todd and decades more experienced. "Use your strength and wear him out," I said.

The match was close, with neither athlete making much ground. The spectators were on their feet. Then came the throw, "Ippon!" the referee shouted. I just about jumped onto the mat cheering. Todd had slammed the black belt to his back and won the match. One of the coaches came up to me and asked, "How did he do it? How did he win?"

"Kettlebells, man, kettlebells," I said.

Later that day at the coaches meeting, a coach whom I had never met brought up Todd. "This guy deserves to be bumped up," he said.

The Ukrainian was later heard to say in broken English, "It was like fighting baby gorilla."

I tell this story to illustrate that you have to fight and compete with what you have at your disposal. It was impossible for Todd to learn decades of technique in a few short months, so he was forced to use the attributes that he did possess. These were strength, power, and stamina—all of which were greatly enhanced through vigorous kettlebell training and mat practice.

Wrestling/Grappling

OFF-SEASON
Weeks 1–4

Three times per week

Figure 8
Kettlebell forward lunge
Kettlebell pass (forward)
Sidewinder
Squat-pull
Squat-press

- *Perform one set each for 10 repetitions.*
- *Add 1 repetition per exercise each workout.*
- *Add weight as you are able.*
- *Drop repetitions back to 10 in Week 4.*
- *Rest 1 to 3 minutes between exercises.*
- *Work through the list of exercises three times, top to bottom.*
- *Rest 3 minutes between cycles.*

Weeks 5–8

Three times per week

Kettlebell pass (all directions)
Side shuffle
Sidewinder
Two-hand swing
Bent-over row
Single press
Single floor press
Squat-pull

- *Perform one set each for 10 repetitions.*
- *Add 1 repetition per exercise each workout.*
- *Add weight as you are able.*
- *Drop repetitions back to 10 in Week 8.*
- *Rest 1 to 3 minutes between exercises.*
- *Work through the list of exercises four times, top to bottom.*
- *Rest 3 minutes between cycles.*

Weeks 9–12

Three times per week

Two-hand swing
Sidewinder
Single snatch
Side shuffle (over step)
Kettlebell pass (all directions)
Double clean
Alternating press-up
Get-up

- *Perform one set each for 10 repetitions.*
- *Add 1 repetition per exercise each workout.*
- *Add weight as you are able.*
- *Drop repetitions back to 10 in Week 12.*
- *Rest 1 to 3 minutes between exercises.*
- *Work through the list of exercises five times, top to bottom.*
- *Rest 3 minutes between cycles.*

PRESEASON

Weeks 1–3

Three times per week

Group 1
Figure 8
Overhead towel swing
Double snatch

Group 2
Single snatch
Double press
One-stays-up row

Group 3
Double clean
Double clean-squat
Double clean-squat-press

- *Perform one set each for 10 repetitions.*
- *Add 1 repetition per exercise each workout.*
- *Add weight as you are able.*
- *Drop repetitions back to 10 in Week 3.*
- *Do not rest between exercises in each group.*
- *Rest 2 minutes between groups.*
- *Work through the list of exercises two times, top to bottom.*

Weeks 4–6

Three times per week

Group 1
Double clean
Side shuffle
Double snatch
Squat-pull

Group 2
Alternating clean
Sidewinder
Kettlebell pass (all directions)
Alternating press-up

Group 3
Squat-press
Single clean
Kettlebell push-up–row
Overhead towel swing

- *Perform one set each for 10 repetitions.*
- *Add 1 repetition per exercise each workout.*
- *Add weight as you are able.*
- *Drop repetitions back to 10 in Week 6.*
- *Do not rest between exercises in each group.*
- *Rest 2 minutes between groups.*
- *Work through the list of exercises two times, top to bottom.*

Weeks 7–9

Three times per week

Group 1
Single clean
Squat-pull
Single snatch
Squat-pull
One-stays-up press
Squat-pull

Group 2
Kettlebell pass (all directions)
Side shuffle (over step)
Alternating clean
Side shuffle (over step)
Kettlebell crawl
Stand-up (from knees)

- *Perform one set each for 10 repetitions.*
- *Add 1 repetition per exercise each workout.*
- *Add weight as you are able.*
- *Drop repetitions back to 10 in Week 9.*
- *Do not rest between exercises in each group.*
- *Rest 2 minutes between groups.*
- *Work through the list of exercises two times, top to bottom.*

Weeks 10–12

Three times per week

Single clean
Sidewinder
One-stays-up row
Squat-pull
One-stays-up press
Double snatch
Alternating press-up

- *Perform one set each for 10 repetitions.*
- *Add 1 repetition per exercise each workout.*
- *Add weight as you are able.*
- *Drop repetitions back to 10 in Week 12.*
- *Do not rest between exercises.*
- *Work through the list of exercises three times, top to bottom.*
- *Rest 2 minutes between cycles.*

IN-SEASON

Weeks 1–3

Two times per week

Overhead towel swing
Single clean
Sidewinder
Kettlebell pass (all directions)
Side shuffle (over step)
Alternating press-up
Get-up
Squat-pull

- *Perform one set each for 5 repetitions.*
- *Add 1 repetition per exercise each workout.*
- *Add weight as you are able.*
- *Drop repetitions back to 5 in Week 3.*
- *Do not rest between exercises.*
- *Work through the list of exercises three times, top to bottom.*
- *Rest 1 minute between cycles.*

Weeks 4–6

Two times per week

Alternating clean
Sidewinder
Squat-pull
Double floor press
Pullover into leg raise (arms extended)
Stand-up (from knees)
Squat-press

- *Perform one set each for 5 repetitions.*
- *Add 1 repetition per exercise each workout.*
- *Add weight as you are able.*
- *Drop repetitions back to 5 in Week 6.*
- *Do not rest between exercises.*
- *Work through the list of exercises three times, top to bottom.*
- *Rest 1 minute between cycles.*

Weeks 7–9

Two times per week

Kettlebell forward lunge
Squat-pull
Kettlebell pass (all directions)
Single clean
Alternating press-up

- *Perform one set each for 5 repetitions.*
- *Add 1 repetition per exercise each workout.*
- *Add weight as you are able.*
- *Drop repetitions back to 5 in Week 9.*
- *Do not rest between exercises.*
- *Work through the list of exercises three times, top to bottom.*
- *Rest 1 minute between cycles.*

Weeks 10–12

Two times per week

Kettlebell pass (all directions)
Sidewinder
Single clean
Double snatch
Kettlebell push-up–row

- *Perform one set each for 5 repetitions.*
- *Add 1 repetition per exercise each workout.*
- *Add weight as you are able.*
- *Drop repetitions back to 5 in Week 12.*
- *Do not rest between exercises.*
- *Work through the list of exercises three times, top to bottom.*
- *Rest 1 minute between cycles.*

POSTSEASON

Week 1

Complete rest

Week 2

Three times per week

Light jogging
Body-weight exercises such as push-ups, chin-ups, crunches,
    light plyometrics, yoga, and stretching

Weeks 3–4

Three times per week

Two-hand swing
One-hand swing
Figure 8
Overhead towel swing
Side bend

- *Perform one set each for 5 repetitions.*
- *Add 1 repetition per exercise each workout.*
- *Add weight as you are able.*
- *Rest 1 to 3 minutes between exercises.*
- *Work through the list of exercises three times, top to bottom.*
- *Rest 3 minutes between cycles.*

Weeks 5–8

Three times per week

Two-hand swing
One-hand swing
Single snatch
Single press
Bent-over row
Side bend
Squat-pull
Side shuffle
Single floor press

- *Perform one set each for 5 repetitions.*
- *Add 1 repetition per exercise each workout.*
- *Add weight as you are able.*
- *Drop repetitions back to 5 in Week 8.*
- *Rest 1 to 3 minutes between exercises.*
- *Work through the list of exercises three times, top to bottom.*
- *Rest 3 minutes between cycles.*

Weeks 9–12

Three times per week

Single snatch
Double clean
Alternating clean
Kettlebell pass (forward)
Kettlebell back lunge
Double floor press into leg raise (arms extended)
Get-up
Single press
Bent-over row
Side bend

- *Perform one set each for 5 repetitions.*
- *Add 1 repetition per exercise each workout.*
- *Add weight as you are able.*
- *Drop repetitions back to 5 in Week 12.*
- *Rest 1 to 3 minutes between exercises.*
- *Work through the list of exercises three times, top to bottom.*
- *Rest 3 minutes between cycles.*

Karate and Striking Sports

OFF-SEASON

Weeks 1–4

Three times per week

Figure 8
Deadlift
Two-hand swing
One-hand swing
Squat-pull
Single press
Bent-over row
Single floor press
Alternating press-up into leg raise
    (arms extended)

- *Perform one set each for 10 repetitions.*
- *Add 1 repetition per exercise each workout.*
- *Drop repetitions back to 10 in Week 4.*
- *Rest 3 minutes between exercises.*
- *Work through the list of exercises three times, top to bottom.*
- *Rest 3 minutes between cycles.*

Weeks 5–8

Four times per week

Figure 8
Overhead towel swing
Deadlift
One-hand swing
Double snatch
Squat-pull
One-stays-up press
One-stays-up row
Alternating press-up
Alternating press-up into leg raise
    (arms extended)
Pullover into leg raise (arms extended)

- *Perform one set each for 10 repetitions.*
- *Add 1 repetition per exercise each workout.*
- *Drop repetitions back to 10 in Week 8.*
- *Rest 3 minutes between exercises.*
- *Work through the list of exercises four times, top to bottom.*
- *Rest 3 minutes between cycles.*

Weeks 9–12

Four times per week

Figure 8
Overhead towel swing
Side bend
Deadlift
One-hand swing
Double snatch
Squat-pull
Double press
Double row
Sidewinder
Alternating press-up
Pullover into leg raise (arms extended)

- *Perform one set each for 10 repetitions.*
- *Add 1 repetition per exercise each workout.*
- *Drop repetitions back to 10 in Week 12.*
- *Rest 3 minutes between exercises.*
- *Work through the list of exercises four times, top to bottom.*
- *Rest 3 minutes between cycles.*

PRESEASON

Weeks 1–4

Four times per week

Group 1
Figure 8
Overhead towel swing
Deadlift

Group 2
Single snatch
Double clean
Double snatch

Group 3
Side shuffle
Squat-pull
Double press
Double row

Group 4
Alternating press-up
Kettlebell push-up–row
Pullover into leg raise (arms extended)

- *Perform one set each for 10 repetitions.*
- *Add 1 repetition per exercise each workout.*
- *Add weight as you are able.*
- *Drop repetitions back to 10 in Week 4.*
- *Do not rest between exercises.*
- *Rest 3 minutes between groups.*
- *Work through the list of exercises four times, top to bottom.*

Four times per week

Group 1
Figure 8
Overhead towel swing
Deadlift

Group 2
Single snatch
Double clean
Double snatch

Group 3
Side shuffle
Squat-pull
One-stays-up press
One-stays-up row

Group 4
Alternating press-up
Kettlebell push-up–row
Pullover into leg raise (arms extended)

Group 5
Kettlebell pass (all directions)
Double clean
One-stays-up press

- *Perform one set each for 10 repetitions.*
- *Add 1 repetition per exercise each workout.*
- *Add weight as you are able.*
- *Drop repetitions back to 10 in Week 8.*
- *Do not rest between exercises.*
- *Rest 3 minutes between groups.*
- *Work through the list of exercises four times, top to bottom.*

Weeks 9–12

Four times per week

Group 1
Figure 8
Overhead towel swing
Deadlift
Sidewinder

Group 2
Single snatch
Single press
Double clean
Double snatch

Group 3
Side shuffle
Squat-pull
Double press
Double row

Group 4
Alternating press-up
Kettlebell push-up–row
Pullover into leg raise (arms extended)

Group 5
Kettlebell pass (all directions)
Double clean
One-stays-up press
Get-up

- *Perform one set each for 10 repetitions.*
- *Add 1 repetition per exercise each workout.*
- *Add weight as you are able.*
- *Drop repetitions back to 10 in Week 12.*
- *Do not rest between exercises.*
- *Rest 3 minutes between groups.*
- *Work through the list of exercises four times, top to bottom.*

IN-SEASON

Weeks 1–4

Two times per week

Group 1
Figure 8
One-hand swing
Single press
Bent-over row

Group 2
Overhead towel swing
Double clean
Kettlebell push-up–row

Group 3
Overhead towel swing
Single snatch
One-stays-up press
One-stays-up row

Group 4
Pullover into leg raise (arms extended)
Single snatch
One-stays-up row
Side shuffle (over step)

Group 5
Kettlebell pass (all directions)
Double clean-squat
Squat-pull
Get-up

- *Perform one set each for 10 repetitions.*
- *Add weight as you are able.*
- *Reduce weight by 20 percent in Week 4.*
- *Do not rest between exercises.*
- *Rest 2 minutes between groups.*
- *Work through the list of exercises three times, top to bottom.*

Two times per week

Group 1
Figure 8
One-hand swing
Single press
Bent-over row

Group 2
Overhead towel swing
Double clean
Kettlebell push-up–row

Group 3
Two-hand swing
Single snatch
Double press
Double row

Group 4
Pullover into leg raise (arms extended)
Double clean
One-stays-up row
Side shuffle (over step)

Group 5
Kettlebell pass (all directions)
Double clean-squat
Squat-pull
Get-up

- *Perform one set each for 10 repetitions.*
- *Add weight as you are able.*
- *Reduce weight by 20 percent in Week 8.*
- *Do not rest between exercises.*
- *Rest 1 minute between groups.*
- *Work through the list of exercises two times, top to bottom.*

Weeks 9–12

Two times per week

Group 1
Figure 8
One-hand swing
Single press
Bent-over row
Overhead towel swing
Double clean

Group 2
Kettlebell push-up–row
Overhead towel swing
Single snatch
Double press
Double row
Pullover into leg raise (arms extended)
Double squat

Group 3
One-stays-up row
Side shuffle (over step)
Kettlebell pass (all directions)
Double clean-squat
Squat-pull
Get-up

- *Perform one set each for 10 repetitions.*
- *Add weight as you are able.*
- *Reduce weight by 20 percent in Week 12.*
- *Do not rest between exercises.*
- *Rest 1 minute between groups.*
- *Work through the list of exercises one time, top to bottom.*

POSTSEASON

Weeks 1–2

Complete rest

Weeks 3–4

Three times per week

Figure 8
Deadlift
Two-hand swing
One-hand swing
Single press
Bent-over row

- *Perform one set each for 10 repetitions.*
- *Add 1 repetition per exercise each workout.*
- *Drop repetitions back to 10 in Week 4.*
- *Rest as much as needed between exercises.*
- *Work through the list of exercises one time, top to bottom.*

Weeks 5–8

Three times per week

Group 1
Side shuffle (with weight)
Overhead towel swing
Alternating clean
Alternating press-up

Group 2
Double swing
Squat-pull
Single snatch
Kettlebell push-up–row

- *Perform one set each for 10 repetitions.*
- *Add 1 repetition per exercise each workout.*
- *Drop repetitions back to 10 in Week 8.*
- *Rest 2 minutes between exercises.*
- *Rest 5 minutes between groups.*
- *Work through the list of exercises one time, top to bottom.*

Weeks 9–12

Three times per week

Group 1
Side shuffle (with weight)
Overhead towel swing
Alternating clean
Alternating press-up

Group 2
Double swing
Squat-pull
Single snatch
Kettlebell push-up–row

Group 3
Double snatch
One-stays-up press
One-stays-up row
Kettlebell pass (all directions)

- *Perform one set each for 10 repetitions.*
- *Add 1 repetition per exercise each workout.*
- *Drop repetitions back to 10 in Week 12.*
- *Rest 2 minutes between exercises.*
- *Rest 5 minutes between groups.*
- *Work through the list of exercises one time, top to bottom.*

SAMPLE PROGRAMS FOR
BASKETBALL AND BASEBALL

13

A few years ago I trained a young basketball player whom we'll call Cassin. He was 265 pounds and just under 7 feet tall. That's right, 7 feet! I came up to his stomach. Like a lot of big guys when they are young, he wasn't forced to move around much or jump a lot because he was so much bigger than the kids he played against. That is a David and Goliath story where Goliath is always winning. Cassin planned on playing basketball for a Division I university. His father and I both shared the concern that Cassin would be a Goliath among Goliaths and a slow one at that.

After giving it some thought, I said to Cassin, "You're big, but so is everyone you will be playing against. These guys not only are big—they are fast, powerful, and very skilled." Some of these guys would, in fact, go on into the NBA. "You need to be strong like a big guy, but fast like a little guy." This seemed to make sense to him, so I designed a kettlebell program that would help Cassin become more explosive and agile.

A lot of really tall guys never learn how to jump properly, because they don't have to early on. They tend to bend at the waist excessively and not fully use the large muscles of their thighs. I wanted him to be able to jump higher by getting him to bend his knees more and to understand the difference between power and strength. He had more than enough strength to perform his required task. What he lacked was power. He was very slow and was not quick at all when moving laterally.

I built Cassin a program that addressed his weaknesses while still enhancing his strengths. It included side shuffles, snatches, swings, cleans, and kettlebell stand-ups, as well as presses, rows, and lots of abdominal work. I am happy to say Cassin progressed extremely well and went on to receive full scholarships in not only basketball but baseball as well. He's a lefty with a 90-mile-an-hour fastball.

Basketball

OFF-SEASON

Weeks 1–4

Three times per week

Deadlift
Squat-pull
Two-hand swing
Single snatch
Single press
Bent-over row
Kettlebell forward lunge
Side shuffle

- *Perform one set each for 10 repetitions.*
- *Add 1 repetition per exercise each workout.*
- *Drop repetitions back to 10 in Week 4.*
- *Rest 3 minutes between exercises.*
- *Work through the list of exercises one time, top to bottom.*

Weeks 5–8

Three times per week

Single snatch
Double clean
Double press
Double row
Kettlebell pass (all directions)
Side shuffle (over step)
Kettlebell forward lunge
Overhead towel swing
Single floor press

- *Perform one set each for 10 repetitions.*
- *Add 1 repetition per exercise each workout.*
- *Drop repetitions back to 10 in Week 8.*
- *Rest 3 minutes between exercises.*
- *Work through the list of exercises two times, top to bottom.*
- *Rest 3 minutes between cycles.*

Weeks 9–12

Three times per week

Figure 8
One-hand swing
Double snatch
Double clean
One-stays-up row
One-stays-up press
Sidewinder
Side shuffle
Kettlebell back lunge
Kettlebell pass (all directions)
Single floor press

- *Perform one set each for 10 repetitions.*
- *Add 1 repetition per exercise each workout.*
- *Drop repetitions back to 10 in Week 12.*
- *Rest 3 minutes between exercises.*
- *Work through the list of exercises three times, top to bottom.*
- *Rest 3 minutes between cycles.*

PRESEASON

Weeks 1–3

Three times per week

Side shuffle (with weight)
Figure 8
Kettlebell pass (all directions)
Double swing
Double snatch
Squat-pull
Sidewinder
Kettlebell back lunge
One-stays-up row
One-stays-up press
Pullover into leg raise (arms extended)
Alternating press-up

- *Perform one set each for 10 repetitions.*
- *Add 1 repetition per exercise each workout.*
- *Add weight as you are able.*
- *Reduce weight and repetitions by 20 percent in Week 3.*
- *Rest 2 minutes between exercises.*
- *Work through the list of exercises three times, top to bottom.*
- *Rest 3 minutes between cycles.*

Weeks 4–6

Three times per week

Side shuffle (with weight)
Figure 8
Kettlebell pass (all directions)
Double swing
Double clean
Double snatch
Squat-pull
Sidewinder
Kettlebell back lunge
One-stays-up row
One-stays-up press
Kettlebell push-up–row
Pullover into leg raise (arms extended)
Alternating press-up

- *Perform one set each for 10 repetitions.*
- *Add 1 repetition per exercise each workout.*
- *Add weight as you are able.*
- *Reduce weight and repetitions by 20 percent in Week 6.*
- *Rest 1 minute between exercises.*
- *Work through the list of exercises three times, top to bottom.*
- *Rest 3 minutes between cycles.*

Weeks 7–9

Three times per week

Side shuffle (with weight)
Figure 8
Overhead towel swing
Kettlebell pass (all directions)
Double swing
Double clean
Double snatch
Squat-pull
Sidewinder
Kettlebell back lunge
One-stays-up row
One-stays-up press
Kettlebell crawl
Kettlebell push-up–row
Pullover into leg raise (arms extended)
Alternating press-up

- *Perform one set each for 10 repetitions.*
- *Add 1 repetition per exercise each workout.*
- *Add weight as you are able.*
- *Reduce weight and repetitions by 20 percent in Week 9.*
- *Do not rest between exercises.*
- *Work through the list of exercises three times, top to bottom.*
- *Rest 3 minutes between cycles.*

Weeks 9–12

Three times per week

Side shuffle (with weight)
Figure 8
Kettlebell pass (all directions)
Double swing
Double snatch
Squat-pull
Sidewinder
Kettlebell back lunge
One-stays-up row
One-stays-up press
Pullover into leg raise (arms extended)
Alternating press-up

- *Perform one set each for 10 repetitions.*
- *Add 1 repetition per exercise each workout.*
- *Add weight as you are able.*
- *Reduce weight and repetitions by 20 percent in Week 12.*
- *Do not rest between exercises.*
- *Work through the list of exercises three times, top to bottom.*
- *Rest 3 minutes between cycles.*

IN-SEASON

Weeks 1–3

Three times per week

Figure 8
Two-hand swing
Double snatch
Double clean
Double clean-squat
Squat-pull
Double press
Get-up
Double floor press into leg raise
    (arms extended)
Alternating press-up into leg raise
    (arms extended)
Alternating press-up
Get-up

- *Perform one set each for 10 repetitions.*
- *Add 1 repetition per exercise each workout.*
- *Add weight as you are able.*
- *Keep repetitions, but reduce weight by 20 percent in Week 3.*
- *Rest 2 minutes between exercises.*
- *Work through the list of exercises two times, top to bottom.*
- *Rest 3 minutes between cycles.*

Weeks 4–6

Three times per week

Figure 8
Two-hand swing
Side shuffle
Kettlebell back lunge
Side shuffle
Double clean
Side shuffle
Kettlebell pass (all directions)
Double press
Double row
Kettlebell push-up–row
Pullover
Double floor press into leg raise
    (arms extended)
Get-up

- *Perform one set each for 10 repetitions.*
- *Add 1 repetition per exercise each workout.*
- *Add weight as you are able.*
- *Keep repetitions, but reduce weight by 20 percent in Week 6.*
- *Rest 1 minute between exercises.*
- *Work through the list of exercises two times, top to bottom.*
- *Rest 3 minutes between cycles.*

Weeks 7–9

Three times per week

Overhead towel swing
One-hand swing
Double snatch
Double clean
Side shuffle
Double clean-squat
Double clean-squat-press
Figure 8
Kettlebell push-up-row
Kettlebell crawl

- *Perform one set each for 10 repetitions.*
- *Add 1 repetition per exercise each workout.*
- *Add weight as you are able.*
- *Keep repetitions, but reduce weight by 20 percent in Week 9.*
- *Do not rest between exercises.*
- *Work through the list of exercises two times, top to bottom.*
- *Rest 3 minutes between cycles.*

Weeks 10–12

Three times per week

Single snatch
Sidewinder
Figure 8
Side shuffle
Double snatch
Alternating clean
Single press
Squat-pull
Bent-over row
Kettlebell pass (all directions)
Side shuffle (over step)

- *Perform one set each for 10 repetitions.*
- *Add 1 repetition per exercise each workout.*
- *Add weight as you are able.*
- *Keep repetitions, but reduce weight by 20 percent in Week 12.*
- *Do not rest between exercises.*
- *Work through the list of exercises one time, top to bottom.*

POSTSEASON

Week 1

Complete rest

Week 2

Four times this week

Light jogging, light plyometrics such as skipping and bounding

Weeks 3–4

Three times per week

Side shuffle (no weight) and light plyometrics
Two-hand swing
Single snatch
Double clean-squat
Overhead towel swing

- *Perform one set each for 5 repetitions.*
- *Add 1 repetition per exercise each workout.*
- *Rest 3 minutes between exercises.*
- *Work through the list of exercises three times, top to bottom.*
- *Rest 3 minutes between cycles.*

Weeks 5–8

Three times per week

Two-hand swing
One-hand swing
Single snatch
Double clean
Single press
Bent-over row
Kettlebell forward lunge
Overhead towel swing

- *Perform one set each for 5 repetitions.*
- *Add 1 repetition per exercise each workout.*
- *Drop repetitions back to 5 in Week 8.*
- *Rest 3 minutes between exercises.*
- *Work through the list of exercises three times, top to bottom.*
- *Rest 3 minutes between cycles.*

Weeks 9–12

Three times per week

Single snatch
Double clean
Double snatch
One-stays-up row
One-stays-up press
Squat-press
Triceps extension (standing)
Kettlebell pass (all directions)
Alternating press-up into leg raise
    (arms extended)
Double floor press into leg raise
    (arms extended)

- *Perform one set each for 5 repetitions.*
- *Add 1 repetition per exercise each workout.*
- *Drop repetitions back to 5 in Week 12.*
- *Rest 3 minutes between exercises.*
- *Work through the list of exercises three times, top to bottom.*
- *Rest 3 minutes between cycles.*

Baseball

OFF-SEASON

Weeks 1–4

Three times per week

Overhead towel swing
Figure 8
Kettlebell back lunge
Side shuffle
Two-hand swing
Single press
Bent-over row (elbow out)
Single floor press

- *Perform one set each for 5 repetitions.*
- *Add 1 repetition per exercise each workout.*
- *Drop repetitions back to 5 in Week 4.*
- *Rest 3 minutes between exercises.*
- *Work through the list of exercises three times, top to bottom.*
- *Rest 3 minutes between cycles.*

Weeks 5–8

Three times per week

Overhead towel swing
Figure 8
One-hand swing
Single snatch
Overhead towel swing
Double press
Double row (elbows out)
Squat-pull
Kettlebell push-up–row
Get-up
Stand-up (from knees)

- *Perform one set each for 7 repetitions.*
- *Add 1 repetition per exercise each workout.*
- *Drop repetitions back to 7 in Week 8.*
- *Rest 3 minutes between exercises.*
- *Work through the list of exercises three times, top to bottom.*
- *Rest 3 minutes between cycles.*

Weeks 9–12

Three times per week

Overhead towel swing
Figure 8
Double snatch
Double clean
Single clean
Alternating clean
One-stays-up press
One-stays-up row (elbows out)
Double press
Kettlebell forward lunge
Side shuffle
Kettlebell pass (all directions)
Alternating press-up into leg raise
    (arms extended)
Pullover into leg raise (arms extended)

- *Perform one set each for 10 repetitions.*
- *Add 1 repetition per exercise each workout.*
- *Drop repetitions back to 10 in Week 12.*
- *Rest 3 minutes between exercises.*
- *Work through the list of exercises three times, top to bottom.*
- *Rest 3 minutes between cycles.*

PRESEASON

Weeks 1–3

Three times per week

Figure 8
One-hand swing
Overhead towel swing
Single snatch
One-stays-up press
One-stays-up row (elbows out)
Double clean
Kettlebell pass (all directions)
Overhead towel swing
Side shuffle
Sidewinder
One-stays-up floor press into leg raise
    (arms extended)

- *Perform one set each for 10 repetitions.*
- *Add 1 repetition per exercise each workout.*
- *Add weight as you are able.*
- *Drop repetitions back to 10 in Week 3.*
- *Rest 3 minutes between exercises.*
- *Work through the list of exercises three times, top to bottom.*
- *Rest 3 minutes between cycles.*

Weeks 4–6

Three times per week

Single floor press
One-stays-up floor press into leg raise
   (arms extended)
Pullover into leg raise (arms extended)
Kettlebell push-up–row
Get-up
Overhead towel swing
Two-hand swing
One-hand swing
Single snatch
Double press
Double row (elbows out)
Alternating clean
Triceps extension (standing)
Overhead towel swing

- *Perform one set each for 10 repetitions.*
- *Add 1 repetition per exercise each workout.*
- *Add weight as you are able.*
- *Drop repetitions back to 10 in Week 6.*
- *Rest 3 minutes between exercises.*
- *Work through the list of exercises three times, top to bottom.*
- *Rest 3 minutes between cycles.*

Weeks 7–9

Three times per week

Kettlebell push-up–row
Kettlebell crawl
Alternating press-up into leg raise
   (arms extended)
One-stays-up floor press into leg raise
   (arms extended)
Pullover into leg raise (arms extended)
Stand-up (from knees)
Side shuffle
Kettlebell forward lunge
Side shuffle (no weight)
Double clean
Double clean-squat
Double row (palms up)
Overhead towel swing

- *Perform one set each for 10 repetitions.*
- *Add 1 repetition per exercise each workout.*
- *Add weight as you are able.*
- *Drop repetitions back to 10 in Week 9.*
- *Rest 3 minutes between exercises.*
- *Work through the list of exercises three times, top to bottom.*
- *Rest 3 minutes between cycles.*

Weeks 10–12

Three times per week

Figure 8
Side bend
Side shuffle (over step)
Kettlebell pass (all directions)
Side shuffle (no weight)
Kettlebell forward lunge
Overhead towel swing
One-hand swing
Single snatch
One-stays-up press
One-stays-up row (elbows out)
Single clean
One-stays-up floor press into leg raise
    (arms extended)
Single floor press
Get-up

- *Perform one set each for 10 repetitions.*
- *Add 1 repetition per exercise each workout.*
- *Add weight as you are able.*
- *Drop repetitions back to 10 in Week 12.*
- *Rest 3 minutes between exercises.*
- *Work through the list of exercises three times, top to bottom.*
- *Rest 3 minutes between cycles.*

IN-SEASON

Weeks 1–3

Two times per week

One-hand swing
Side shuffle
Overhead towel swing
Kettlebell push-up–row
Kettlebell pass
Double clean-squat
Double clean-squat-press
Kettlebell forward lunge
Stand-up (from knees)
Get-up

- *Perform one set each for 5 repetitions.*
- *Add 1 repetition per exercise each workout.*
- *Add weight as you are able.*
- *Drop repetitions back to 5 in Week 3.*
- *Rest 2 minutes between exercises.*
- *Work through the list of exercises three times, top to bottom.*
- *Rest 2 minutes between cycles.*

Weeks 4–6

Two times per week

Two-hand swing
One-hand swing
Kettlebell pass (all directions)
Kettlebell forward lunge
Single snatch
Double press
Double row
Squat-pull
Sidewinder
Overhead towel swing
Kettlebell push-up–row
Pullover into leg raise (arms extended)

- *Perform one set each for 5 repetitions.*
- *Add 1 repetition per exercise each workout.*
- *Add weight as you are able.*
- *Drop repetitions back to 5 in Week 6.*
- *Rest 2 minutes between exercises.*
- *Work through the list of exercises two times, top to bottom.*
- *Rest 2 minutes between cycles.*

Weeks 7–9

Two times per week

Figure 8
Side bend
Overhead towel swing
Side shuffle (over step)
One-hand swing
Double snatch
Alternating clean
One-stays-up press
One-stays-up row (elbows out)
Kettlebell back lunge
Double floor press into leg raise (arms extended)
Alternating press-up into leg raise
    (arms extended)

- *Perform one set each for 5 repetitions.*
- *Add 1 repetition per exercise each workout.*
- *Add weight as you are able.*
- *Drop repetitions back to 5 in Week 9.*
- *Rest 1 minute between exercises.*
- *Work through the list of exercises one time, top to bottom.*

Weeks 10–12

Two times per week

Kettlebell pass (all directions)
Side shuffle (over step)
One-hand swing
Single snatch
Side shuffle (no weight)
Alternating clean
Double clean-squat
Kettlebell forward lunge
Double row (elbows out)
Double press
Kettlebell push-up–row
Kettlebell crawl
Walking swing (two hands)

- *Perform one set each for 5 repetitions.*
- *Add 1 repetition per exercise each workout.*
- *Add weight as you are able.*
- *Drop repetitions back to 5 in Week 12.*
- *Do not rest between exercises.*
- *Work through the list of exercises one time, top to bottom.*

POSTSEASON

Week 1

Complete rest

Weeks 2–4

Three times per week

Stretch band work: internal and external
   shoulder rotation, flexion and extension
   at shoulder, etc.
Figure 8
Two-hand swing
Side shuffle (no weight)
One-hand swing
Overhead towel swing
Single press
Bent-over row

- *Perform one set each for 5 repetitions.*
- *Add 1 repetition per exercise each workout.*
- *Rest 3 minutes between exercises.*
- *Work through the list of exercises one time, top to bottom.*

Weeks 5–8

Three times per week

Stretch band work: internal and external
shoulder rotation, flexion and extension
at shoulder, etc.
Figure 8
Two-hand swing
Side shuffle (no weight)
One-hand swing
Overhead towel swing
One-stays-up press
One-stays-up row
Squat-pull

- *Perform one set each for 5 repetitions.*
- *Add 1 repetition per exercise each workout.*
- *Drop repetitions back to 5 in Week 8.*
- *Rest 3 minutes between exercises.*
- *Work through the list of exercises two times, top to bottom.*
- *Rest 3 minutes between cycles.*

Weeks 9–12

Three times per week

Stretch band work: internal and external
shoulder rotation, flexion and extension
at shoulder, etc.
Figure 8
Two-hand swing
Double clean
Side shuffle (no weight)
One-hand swing
Overhead towel swing
One-stays-up press
One-stays-up row
Squat-pull
Sidewinder

- *Perform one set each for 5 repetitions.*
- *Add 1 repetition per exercise each workout.*
- *Drop repetitions back to 5 in Week 12.*
- *Rest 3 minutes between exercises.*
- *Work through the list of exercises three times, top to bottom.*
- *Rest 3 minutes between cycles.*

SAMPLE PROGRAMS FOR
TRACK-AND-FIELD SPRINTERS, LONG-DISTANCE RUNNERS, AND THROWERS

14

About a year ago I received a kettlebell order from a gentleman who was a masters division sprinter. He was living in a neighboring town to work on his graduate degree and said he would like to pick up his kettlebell instead of having it shipped. I told him I would be glad to give him a quick lesson, and he said that would be great. Based upon his order of a 145-pound weight, I correctly assumed he had quite a bit of experience training with kettlebells. He looked more like a college linebacker than a sprinter.

We talked about technique, and I shared my opinions on several key lifts. He then told me an interesting story about his personal conditioning program. He had previously used conventional strength-training techniques to help his sprinting. Among those exercises were barbell squats and other big multi-joint leg movements. He decided to give kettlebell training a try and gave up his squats. He experienced a slight loss of size in his thighs, but his sprinting times improved. He wasn't quite sure why, but he liked his results.

The reason I offered was this: sprinting and other types of running are mainly focused around the hip. People do not completely flex and extend the knee when running. Athletes sometimes place too much emphasis on developing the musculature around the knee and become thigh heavy. What they should be doing is working more on the musculature around the hip so they are able to execute faster strides. Kettlebell swings, snatches, and cleans all work the hips extensively while still working the range of motion in the knee that is necessary for running.

For each exercise, follow the recommended repetition scheme, unless otherwise noted in parentheses.

Sprinters

OFF-SEASON

Weeks 1–4

Three times per week

Two-hand swing
Kettlebell forward lunge
Double clean
Alternating clean
Double floor press into leg raise
(arms extended)

- *Perform one set each for 5 repetitions.*
- *Add 1 repetition per exercise each workout.*
- *Drop repetitions back to 5 in Week 4.*
- *Rest 3 minutes between exercises.*
- *Work through the list of exercises three times, top to bottom.*
- *Rest 3 minutes between cycles.*

Week 5–8

Three times per week

Two-hand swing
One-hand swing
Overhead towel swing
Kettlebell forward lunge
Kettlebell back lunge
Double clean
Alternating clean
Double floor press into leg raise
(arms extended)

- *Perform one set each for 7 repetitions.*
- *Add 1 repetition per exercise each workout.*
- *Drop repetitions back to 7 in Week 8.*
- *Rest 3 minutes between exercises.*
- *Work through the list of exercises three times, top to bottom.*
- *Rest 3 minutes between cycles.*

Weeks 9–12

Three times per week

Two-hand swing
One-hand swing
Overhead towel swing
Double clean
Double squat
Double press
Double row (elbows out)
Kettlebell forward lunge
Double floor press into leg raise
(arms extended)

- *Perform one set each for 10 repetitions.*
- *Add 1 repetition per exercise each workout.*
- *Drop repetitions back to 10 in Week 12.*
- *Rest 3 minutes between exercises.*
- *Work through the list of exercises three times, top to bottom.*
- *Rest 3 minutes between cycles.*

PRESEASON

Weeks 1–3

Three times per week

Overhead towel swing
One-hand swing
Double clean
Double squat
Double press
Double row (elbows out)
Kettlebell forward lunge
Double floor press into leg raise
    (arms extended)

- *Perform one set each for 10 repetitions.*
- *Add 1 repetition per exercise each workout.*
- *Add weight as you are able.*
- *Drop repetitions back to 10 in Week 3.*
- *Reduce weight by 20 percent in Week 3.*
- *Rest 3 minutes between exercises.*
- *Work through the list of exercises three times, top to bottom.*
- *Rest 3 minutes between cycles.*

Weeks 4–6

Three times per week

Overhead towel swing
One-hand swing
Double clean
Double squat
Double swing
Double press
Double row (elbows out)
Double swing
Kettlebell forward lunge
Double floor press into leg raise
    (arms extended)

- *Perform one set each for 10 repetitions.*
- *Add 1 repetition per exercise each workout.*
- *Add weight as you are able.*
- *Drop repetitions back to 10 in Week 6.*
- *Reduce weight by 20 percent in Week 6.*
- *Rest 3 minutes between exercises.*
- *Work through the list of exercises three times, top to bottom.*
- *Rest 3 minutes between cycles.*

Weeks 7–9

Three times per week

Overhead towel swing
One-hand swing
Two-hand swing
Double squat
Double swing
Hammer curl
Double press
Double row (elbows out)
Single snatch
Kettlebell forward lunge
Double floor press into leg raise
    (arms extended)
Pullover into leg raise (arms extended)

- *Perform one set each for 10 repetitions.*
- *Add 1 repetition per exercise each workout.*
- *Add weight as you are able.*
- *Drop repetitions back to 10 in Week 9.*
- *Reduce weight by 20 percent in Week 9.*
- *Rest 3 minutes between exercises.*
- *Work through the list of exercises three times, top to bottom.*
- *Rest 3 minutes between cycles.*

Weeks 10–12

Three times per week

Overhead towel swing
Two-hand swing
Figure 8
Double squat
Double swing
Hammer curl
Triceps extension (standing)
Double press
Double row (elbows out)
Kettlebell forward lunge
Double snatch
Double floor press into leg raise
    (arms extended)
Pullover into leg raise (arms extended)

- *Perform one set each for 10 repetitions.*
- *Add 1 repetition per exercise each workout.*
- *Add weight as you are able.*
- *Drop repetitions back to 10 in Week 12.*
- *Reduce weight by 20 percent in Week 12.*
- *Rest 3 minutes between exercises.*
- *Work through the list of exercises three times, top to bottom.*
- *Rest 3 minutes between cycles.*

IN-SEASON

Weeks 1–4

Three times per week

Figure 8
Two-hand swing
Double press
Double row (elbows out)
Hammer curl
Triceps extension (standing)
Double snatch
Kettlebell forward lunge
Two-hand swing
Alternating press-up into leg raise
    (arms extended)
Pullover into leg raise (arms extended)

- *Perform one set each for 10 repetitions.*
- *Add weight as you are able.*
- *Reduce weight by 20 percent in Week 4.*
- *Rest 3 minutes between exercises.*
- *Work through the list of exercises three times, top to bottom.*
- *Rest 3 minutes between cycles.*

Weeks 5–8

Three times per week

Figure 8
Side bend
Two-hand swing
Double press
Double row (elbows out)
Hammer curl
Triceps extension (standing)
Double snatch
Kettlebell forward lunge
Alternating press-up into leg raise
    (arms extended)
Pullover into leg raise (arms extended)

- *Perform one set each for 7 repetitions.*
- *Add weight as you are able.*
- *Reduce weight by 20 percent in Week 8.*
- *Rest 3 minutes between exercises.*
- *Work through the list of exercises three times, top to bottom.*
- *Rest 3 minutes between cycles.*

Weeks 9–12

Three times per week

Figure 8
Side bend
Overhead towel swing
Two-hand swing
One-stays-up press
Double row (elbows out)
Double swing
Alternating press-up into leg raise
    (arms extended)
Pullover into leg raise (arms extended)

- *Perform one set each for 5 repetitions.*
- *Add weight as you are able.*
- *Reduce weight by 20 percent in Week 12.*
- *Rest 3 minutes between exercises.*
- *Work through the list of exercises three times, top to bottom.*
- *Rest 3 minutes between cycles.*

POSTSEASON

Week 1

Complete rest

Week 2

Three times this week

Stretching and light plyometrics

Weeks 3–4

Three times per week

Figure 8
Pullover into leg raise (arms extended)
Alternating press-up
Get-up
Bent-over row
Single press
Squat-pull

- *Perform one set each for 5 repetitions.*
- *Add 1 repetition per exercise each workout.*
- *Rest 3 minutes between exercises.*
- *Work through the list of exercises three times, top to bottom.*
- *Rest 3 minutes between cycles.*

Three times per week

Figure 8
One-hand swing
Kettlebell pass
Pullover into leg raise (arms extended)
Alternating press-up
Get-up
Kettlebell back lunge
Bent-over row
Single press
Squat-pull

- *Perform one set each for 7 repetitions.*
- *Add 1 repetition per exercise each workout.*
- *Drop repetitions back to 7 in Week 8.*
- *Rest 3 minutes between exercises.*
- *Work through the list of exercises three times, top to bottom.*
- *Rest 3 minutes between cycles.*

Three times per week

Figure 8
Overhead towel swing
One-hand swing
Single snatch
Kettlebell pass
Pullover into leg raise (arms extended)
Alternating press-up
Get-up
Kettlebell back lunge
Double row
Double press
Squat-pull
Sidewinder

- *Perform one set each for 7 repetitions.*
- *Add 1 repetition per exercise each workout.*
- *Drop repetitions back to 7 in Week 12.*
- *Rest 3 minutes between exercises.*
- *Work through the list of exercises three times, top to bottom.*
- *Rest 3 minutes between cycles.*

Long-Distance Runners

OFF-SEASON

Weeks 1–4

Three times per week

Figure 8
Overhead towel swing
Deadlift
One-hand swing
Two-hand swing
Kettlebell pass
Pullover into leg raise (arms extended)
Alternating press-up

- *Perform one set each for 5 repetitions.*
- *Add 1 repetition per exercise each workout.*
- *Drop repetitions back to 5 in Week 4.*
- *Rest 3 minutes between exercises.*
- *Work through the list of exercises three times, top to bottom.*
- *Rest 3 minutes between cycles.*

Weeks 5–8

Three times per week

Figure 8
Overhead towel swing
Deadlift
One-hand swing
Two-hand swing
Single snatch
Kettlebell pass
Single press
Bent-over row
Pullover into leg raise (arms extended)
Alternating press-up

- *Perform one set each for 7 repetitions.*
- *Add 1 repetition per exercise each workout.*
- *Drop repetitions back to 7 in Week 8.*
- *Rest 2 minutes between exercises.*
- *Work through the list of exercises three times, top to bottom.*
- *Rest 3 minutes between cycles.*

Weeks 9–12

Three times per week

Figure 8
Overhead towel swing
Pullover into leg raise (arms extended)
Alternating press-up
Deadlift
One-hand swing
Two-hand swing
Single snatch
Kettlebell forward lunge
Kettlebell pass
Double press
Double row

- *Perform one set each for 10 repetitions.*
- *Add 1 repetition per exercise each workout.*
- *Drop repetitions back to 10 in Week 12.*
- *Rest 1 minute between exercises.*
- *Work through the list of exercises three times, top to bottom.*
- *Rest 3 minutes between cycles.*

PRESEASON

Weeks 1–3

Three times per week

Figure 8
Overhead towel swing
Pullover into leg raise (arms extended)
Alternating press-up
Deadlift
One-hand swing
Two-hand swing
Single snatch
Kettlebell forward lunge
Kettlebell pass
Side shuffle
Double press
Double row

- *Perform one set each for 12 repetitions.*
- *Add 1 repetition per exercise each workout.*
- *Drop repetitions back to 12 in Week 3.*
- *Rest 1 minute between exercises.*
- *Work through the list of exercises three times, top to bottom.*
- *Rest 3 minutes between cycles.*

Weeks 4–6

Three times per week

Deadlift
One-hand swing
Two-hand swing
Single snatch
Side shuffle
Kettlebell forward lunge
Kettlebell pass
Side shuffle
Double press
Double row
Sidewinder

- *Perform one set each for 15 repetitions.*
- *Add 1 repetition per exercise each workout.*
- *Drop repetitions back to 15 in Week 6.*
- *Rest 1 minute between exercises.*
- *Work through the list of exercises three times, top to bottom.*
- *Rest 3 minutes between cycles.*

Weeks 7–9

Three times per week

Two-hand swing
Single snatch
Side shuffle
Kettlebell forward lunge
Kettlebell pass
Side shuffle
Double press
Double row (elbows out)
Sidewinder

- *Perform one set each for 17 repetitions.*
- *Add 1 repetition per exercise each workout.*
- *Add weight as you are able.*
- *Drop repetitions back to 17 in Week 9.*
- *Rest 1 minute between exercises.*
- *Work through the list of exercises three times, top to bottom.*
- *Rest 3 minutes between cycles.*

Weeks 10–12

Three times per week

Two-hand swing
Single snatch
Side shuffle
Kettlebell forward lunge
Side shuffle
Double press
Double row (elbows out)
Kettlebell back lunge

- *Perform one set each for 20 repetitions.*
- *Add 1 repetition per exercise each workout.*
- *Add weight as you are able.*
- *Drop repetitions back to 20 in Week 12.*
- *Rest 1 minute between exercises.*
- *Work through the list of exercises three times, top to bottom.*
- *Rest 3 minutes between cycles.*

IN-SEASON

Weeks 1–4

Two times per week

Two-hand swing
Squat-pull
Squat-press
Kettlebell forward lunge
Side shuffle (over step)
Pullover into leg raise (arms extended)
Alternating press-up

- *Perform one set each for 25 repetitions.*
- *Add 1 repetition per exercise each workout.*
- *Drop repetitions back to 25 in Week 4.*
- *Do not rest between exercises.*
- *Work through the list of exercises three times, top to bottom.*
- *Rest 3 minutes between cycles.*

Weeks 5–8

Two times per week

Two-hand swing
Squat-pull
Squat-press
Side shuffle (over step)
Pullover into leg raise (arms extended)
Alternating press-up

- *Perform one set each for 30 repetitions.*
- *Add 1 repetition per exercise each workout.*
- *Drop repetitions back to 30 in Week 8.*
- *Do not rest between exercises.*
- *Work through the list of exercises three times, top to bottom.*
- *Rest 3 minutes between cycles.*

Weeks 9–10

Two times per week

Two-hand swing
One-hand swing
Sidewinder
Side shuffle (over step)
Pullover into leg raise (arms extended)

- *Perform one set each for 50 repetitions.*
- *Add 1 repetition per exercise each workout.*
- *Do not rest between exercises.*
- *Work through the list of exercises three times, top to bottom.*
- *Rest 3 minutes between cycles.*

Weeks 11–12

No strength training

POSTSEASON

Weeks 1–4

Three times per week

Figure 8
Two-hand swing
Single press
Bent-over row

- *Perform one set each for 20 repetitions.*
- *Add 1 repetition per exercise each workout.*
- *Add weight as you are able.*
- *Reduce weight and repetitions by 20 percent in Week 4.*
- *Rest as much as needed between exercises.*
- *Work through the list of exercises one time, top to bottom.*

Weeks 5–8

Three times per week

Side shuffle (with weight)
Squat-pull
Figure 8
Two-hand swing
Single snatch
One-stays-up row
One-stays-up press

- *Perform one set each for 25 repetitions.*
- *Add 1 repetition per exercise each workout.*
- *Add weight as you are able.*
- *Reduce weight and repetitions by 20 percent in Week 8.*
- *Rest as much as needed between exercises.*
- *Work through the list of exercises one time, top to bottom.*

Weeks 9–12

Three times per week

Kettlebell back lunge
Side shuffle (with weight)
Kettlebell pass (all directions)
Two-hand swing
Squat-pull
Sidewinder
Bent-over row
Alternating press-up
Pullover into leg raise (arms extended)

- *Perform one set each for 30 repetitions.*
- *Add 1 repetition per exercise each workout.*
- *Add weight as you are able.*
- *Reduce weight and repetitions by 20 percent in Week 12.*
- *Rest as much as needed between exercises.*
- *Work through the list of exercises one time, top to bottom.*

Throwers

OFF-SEASON

Weeks 1–4

Three times per week

Figure 8
Overhead towel swing
Two-hand swing
One-hand swing
Double clean
Squat-pull
Single press

- *Perform one set each for 5 repetitions.*
- *Add 1 repetition per exercise each workout.*
- *Drop repetitions back to 5 in Week 4.*
- *Rest 3 minutes between exercises.*
- *Work through the list of exercises three times, top to bottom.*
- *Rest 3 minutes between cycles.*

Weeks 5–8

Three times per week

Figure 8
One-hand swing
Overhead towel swing
Double clean
Overhead towel swing
Single snatch
Squat-pull
Single floor press
Pullover into leg raise (arms extended)

- *Perform one set each for 5 repetitions.*
- *Add 1 repetition per exercise each workout.*
- *Drop repetitions back to 5 in Week 8.*
- *Rest 3 minutes between exercises.*
- *Work through the list of exercises four times, top to bottom.*
- *Rest 3 minutes between cycles.*

Weeks 9–12

Three times per week

One-hand swing
Single snatch
Double clean
Double clean-squat
Double clean-squat-press
Bent-over row
Alternating press-up
Double floor press into leg raise
    (arms extended)
Overhead towel swing

- *Perform one set each for 5 repetitions.*
- *Add 1 repetition per exercise each workout.*
- *Drop repetitions back to 5 in Week 12.*
- *Rest 3 minutes between exercises.*
- *Work through the list of exercises five times, top to bottom.*
- *Rest 3 minutes between cycles.*

PRESEASON

Weeks 1–4

Three times per week

Figure 8
Overhead towel swing
Single snatch
Double clean
Single press
Bent-over row
Double floor press
Squat-press

- *Perform one set each for 5 repetitions.*
- *Add weight as you are able.*
- *Reduce weight by 20 percent in Week 4.*
- *Rest 3 minutes between exercises.*
- *Work through the list of exercises five times, top to bottom.*
- *Rest 3 minutes between cycles.*

Weeks 5–8

Three times per week

Figure 8
Overhead towel swing
Single snatch
Double clean
Double snatch
Single press
Bent-over row
Squat-pull
Double floor press
Squat-press

- *Perform one set each for 5 repetitions.*
- *Add weight as you are able.*
- *Reduce weight by 20 percent in Week 8.*
- *Rest 3 minutes between exercises.*
- *Work through the list of exercises five times, top to bottom.*
- *Rest 3 minutes between cycles.*

Weeks 9–12

Three times per week

Figure 8
Overhead towel swing
Single snatch
Double clean
Double snatch
Single press
Bent-over row
Squat-pull
Kettlebell crawl
Double floor press
Alternating press-up
Squat-press

- *Perform one set each for 5 repetitions.*
- *Add weight as you are able.*
- *Reduce weight by 20 percent in Week 12.*
- *Rest 3 minutes between exercises.*
- *Work through the list of exercises five times, top to bottom.*
- *Rest 3 minutes between cycles.*

IN-SEASON

Weeks 1–3

Three times per week

Figure 8 (10)
Overhead towel swing (10)
Double swing
Double snatch
Double clean
Double clean-squat
Double row (elbows out)
Alternating press-up
One-stays-up floor press into leg raise
    (arms extended)

- *Perform one set each for 5 repetitions.*
- *Add weight as you are able.*
- *Reduce weight by 20 percent in Week 3.*
- *Rest 3 minutes between exercises.*
- *Work through the list of exercises three times, top to bottom.*
- *Rest 3 minutes between cycles.*

Weeks 4–6

Three times per week

Figure 8 (10)
Overhead towel swing (10)
Double snatch
Double clean
Double clean-squat-press
Double row (elbows out)
Alternating press-up
One-stays-up floor press into leg raise
    (arms extended)

- *Perform one set each for 5 repetitions.*
- *Add weight as you are able.*
- *Reduce weight by 20 percent in Week 6.*
- *Rest 3 minutes between exercises.*
- *Work through the list of exercises three times, top to bottom.*
- *Rest 3 minutes between cycles.*

Weeks 7–9

Two times per week

Figure 8 (10)
Overhead towel swing (10)
Double snatch
Double clean-squat-press
Double row (elbows out) (5)
Alternating press-up
One-stays-up floor press into leg raise
    (arms extended)

- *Perform one set each for 3 repetitions.*
- *Add weight as you are able.*
- *Reduce weight by 20 percent in Week 9.*
- *Rest 3 minutes between exercises.*
- *Work through the list of exercises three times, top to bottom.*
- *Rest 3 minutes between cycles.*

Weeks 10–12

Two times per week

Figure 8 (10)
Overhead towel swing (10)
Double snatch
Double clean-squat-press
Double row (elbows out) (5)
Alternating press-up
One-stays-up floor press into leg raise
(arms extended)

- *Perform one set each for 3 repetitions.*
- *Add weight as you are able.*
- *Reduce weight by 20 percent in Week 12.*
- *Rest 3 minutes between exercises.*
- *Work through the list of exercises three times, top to bottom.*
- *Rest 3 minutes between cycles.*

POSTSEASON

Week 1

Complete rest

Week 2

Three times this week

Light plyometrics such as skipping and
bounding as well as body-weight
calisthenics and abdominal work

Weeks 3–4

Three times per week

Deadlift
Squat-pull
Squat-press
Two-hand swing
Overhead towel swing

- *Perform one set each for 5 repetitions.*
- *Add 1 repetition per exercise each workout.*
- *Rest 3 minutes between exercises.*
- *Work through the list of exercises three times, top to bottom.*
- *Rest 3 minutes between cycles.*

Weeks 5–8

Three times per week

One-hand swing
Single snatch
Double clean
Squat-pull
Single press
Bent-over row
Overhead towel swing
Single floor press

- *Perform one set each for 5 repetitions.*
- *Add 1 repetition per exercise each workout.*
- *Add weight as you are able.*
- *Drop repetitions back to 5 in Week 8.*
- *Rest 3 minutes between exercises.*
- *Work through the list of exercises three times, top to bottom.*
- *Rest 3 minutes between cycles.*

Weeks 9–12

Three times per week

Single snatch
Double clean
Double snatch
Double clean-squat-press
Alternating press-up
Pullover into leg raise (arms extended)
Overhead towel swing
Get-up

- *Perform one set each for 5 repetitions.*
- *Add 1 repetition per exercise each workout.*
- *Add weight as you are able.*
- *Drop repetitions back to 5 in Week 12.*
- *Rest 3 minutes between exercises.*
- *Work through the list of exercises three times, top to bottom.*
- *Rest 3 minutes between cycles.*

TOTAL CONDITIONING FOR MILITARY, FIRE, AND LAW-ENFORCEMENT PERSONNEL

15

I have trained many military, fire, and law-enforcement personnel over the years, but one soldier in particular comes to mind. For security reasons, we'll call him Mark. Mark was a career soldier in the Special Forces and bravely served in Afghanistan, Iraq, and other places around the world. He was in his early thirties and very fit. He wanted to improve his physical fitness scores, which were already excellent to begin with.

I said to him, "Let me show you something that is completely different from anything you have ever done. If you don't like it, I won't bring it up again." Mark, always up for a challenge, agreed. I taught him basic kettlebell posture, then two-hand swings, one-hand swings, snatches, double cleans, kettlebell presses and rows, and squat-pulls. Mark was completely drenched with perspiration. With his hands on his knees, breathing loudly and chest heaving, he said, "That was awesome! We definitely need to bring that workout back to my team."

I said, "That was just technique and warm-up—the workout hasn't started yet."

I worked with Mark for a month while he was on leave, and not only did his general physical conditioning improve with kettlebell training, but so did his physical fitness scores. We used the kettlebells, in conjunction with particular body-weight exercises, to get Mark used to working at a higher heart rate. This greatly reduced his overall fatigue when running and helped give him more muscular endurance for chin-ups, push-ups, and sit-ups.

I use Mark as an example to illustrate how kettlebells can be used as tools to condition anyone who desires to improve his or her physical condition. Soldiers, firefighters, and police officers bravely serve every day. Although what such people do professionally transcends sport, I want to address the conditioning that would enhance their physical job performance. These men and women are usually forced to look for advanced physical conditioning information in fitness magazines, but those articles are usually not written with them in mind.

Here is a sample of a training program that can give soldiers, firefighters, and police officials some direction in designing their own programs. Follow the same set and repetition scheme for each exercise, unless otherwise noted in parentheses. For timed exercises, perform as many repetitions as possible within the allotted time.

Basic Training: Avoid Local Fatigue, Build Volume

Weeks 1–4

Three days per week

Figure 8 (20)
Side bend (5 each side)
Deadlift
Two-hand swing
One-hand swing
Single snatch
Chin-up (5)
Single press
Bent-over row
Push-up (1 minute)
Sit-up (1 minute)

- *Perform one set each for 10 repetitions.*
- *Add 1 repetition per exercise each workout.*
- *Reduce weight, repetitions, or both by 20 percent in Week 4.*
- *Rest 3 minutes between exercises.*
- *Work through the list of exercises one time, top to bottom.*

Weeks 5–8

Three days per week

Figure 8 (20)
Side bend (5 each side)
Two-hand swing
One-hand swing
Single snatch
Chin-up (5)
Double clean
Single press
Kettlebell forward lunge
Bent-over row
Squat-thrust (1 minute)
Push-up (1 minute)
Sit-up (1 minute)

- *Perform 1 set each for 10 repetitions.*
- *Add 1 repetition per exercise each workout.*
- *Reduce weight, repetitions, or both by 20 percent in Week 8.*
- *Rest 3 minutes between exercises.*
- *Work through the list of exercises two times, top to bottom.*
- *Rest 3 minutes between cycles.*

Weeks 9–12

Three days per week

Overhead towel swing (20 each side)
Side bend (5 each side)
One-hand swing
Single snatch
Chin-up (5)
Double clean
Single press
Alternating clean
Kettlebell forward lunge
Bent-over row
Kettlebell pass (forward)
Squat-press
Squat-thrust (1 minute)
Push-up (1 minute)
Sit-up (1 minute)

- *Perform one set each for 10 repetitions.*
- *Add 1 repetition per exercise each workout.*
- *Reduce weight, repetitions, or both by 20 percent in Week 12.*
- *Rest 3 minutes between exercises.*
- *Work through the list of exercises three times, top to bottom.*
- *Rest 3 minutes between cycles.*

Advanced Conditioning: Moderate Intensity/High Volume

Weeks 1–4

Three days per week

Overhead towel swing
Single snatch
Push-up
Chin-up
Double floor press into leg raise
  (arms extended)
Double snatch
Double press
Double row
Side shuffle
Alternating clean
Kettlebell forward lunge
Kettlebell pass (all directions)
Sidewinder
Squat-thrust (1½ minutes)
Sit-up (1½ minutes)

- *Perform one set each for 10 repetitions.*
- *Add 1 repetition per exercise each workout.*
- *Reduce weight, repetitions, or both by 20 percent in Week 4.*
- *Rest 2 minutes between exercises.*
- *Work through the list of exercises three times, top to bottom.*
- *Rest 3 minutes between cycles.*

Weeks 5–8

Four days per week

Single snatch
Alternating press-up
Chin-up
Double floor press into leg raise
  (arms extended)
Double snatch
Double press
Double clean-squat
Double row
Side shuffle
Alternating clean
Kettlebell forward lunge
Kettlebell pass (all directions)
Sidewinder
Squat-thrust (1½ minutes)
Sit-up (1½ minutes)

- *Perform one set each for 10 repetitions.*
- *Add 1 repetition per exercise each workout.*
- *Reduce weight, repetitions, or both by 20 percent in Week 8.*
- *Rest 1 minute between exercises.*
- *Work through the list of exercises three times, top to bottom.*
- *Rest 3 minutes between cycles.*

Weeks 9–12

Four days per week

Weighted chin-up (5)
Two-hand swing
Double swing
Double press
Double snatch
Double row
Side shuffle (over step) (20)
Sidewinder
Alternating press-up into leg raise
    (arms extended)
Squat-pull

- *Perform one set each for 10 repetitions.*
- *Add 1 repetition per exercise each workout.*
- *Reduce weight, repetitions, or both by 20 percent in Week 12.*
- *Do not rest between exercises.*
- *Work through the list of exercises three times, top to bottom.*
- *Rest 3 minutes between cycles.*

Fighting Fit:
High Intensity/Moderate Volume

Weeks 1–3

Three days per week

Double clean-squat
Squat-thrust (2 minutes)
Weighted chin-up (5)
Squat-pull
Sit-up (2 minutes)
Kettlebell pass
Side shuffle (20)

- *Perform one set each for 10 repetitions.*
- *Increase resistance by 5 to 10 percent as you are able.*
- *Add 1 repetition per exercise each workout.*
- *Reduce weight, repetitions, or both by 20 percent in Week 3.*
- *Do not rest between exercises.*
- *Work through the list of exercises three times, top to bottom.*
- *Rest 3 minutes between cycles.*

Weeks 4–6

Three days per week

Double clean-squat
Squat-thrust (2 minutes)
Push-up (2 minutes)
Alternating floor press into leg raise
    (arms extended)
Squat-pull
Sit-up (2 minutes)
Kettlebell pass
Side shuffle (20)

- *Perform one set each for 10 repetitions.*
- *Increase resistance by 5 to 10 percent as you are able.*
- *Add 1 repetition per exercise each workout.*
- *Reduce weight, repetitions, or both by 20 percent in Week 6.*
- *Do not rest between exercises.*
- *Work through the list of exercises three times, top to bottom.*
- *Rest 3 minutes between cycles.*

Weeks 7–9

Three days per week

Double clean-squat
Squat-thrust (2 minutes)
Weighted chin-up (5)
Alternating floor press into leg raise
    (arms extended) (start at 20 sweeps each
    side)
Squat-pull
Kettlebell push-up–row
Sit-up (2 minutes)
Kettlebell pass
Side shuffle
Kettlebell crawl
Squat-thrust (2 minutes)

- *Perform one set each for 10 repetitions.*
- *Increase resistance by 5 to 10 percent as you are able.*
- *Add 1 repetition per exercise each workout.*
- *Reduce weight, repetitions, or both by 20 percent in Week 9.*
- *Do not rest between exercises.*
- *Work through the list of exercises three times, top to bottom.*
- *Rest 3 minutes between cycles.*

Weeks 10–12

Three days per week

Alternating clean
One-stays-up press
Squat-thrust (2 minutes)
Weighted chin-up
Alternating floor press into leg raise
    (arms extended)
Push-up (2 minutes)
Squat-pull
Kettlebell push-up–row
Sit-up (2 minutes)
Kettlebell pass
Side shuffle
Kettlebell crawl
Yoga plank (for time)

- *Perform one set each for 10 repetitions.*
- *Increase resistance by 5 to 10 percent as you are able.*
- *Add 1 repetition per exercise each workout.*
- *Reduce weight, repetitions, or both by 20 percent in Week 12.*
- *Do not rest between exercises.*
- *Work through the list of exercises three times, top to bottom.*
- *Rest 3 minutes between cycles.*

R&R: Low Intensity/Low Volume

Weeks 1–2

Complete rest

Weeks 3–4

Three days per week

One-hand swing
Figure 8
Side bend (5 each side)
Kettlebell pass (all directions)
Single snatch
Single press
Bent-over row

- *Perform one set each for 10 repetitions.*
- *Add 1 repetition per exercise each workout.*
- *Rest 3 minutes between exercises.*
- *Work through the list of exercises one time, top to bottom.*

Weeks 5–8

Three days per week

One-hand swing
Double press
Double row
Single snatch
Push-up
Squat-pull
Overhead towel swing
Figure 8

- *Perform one set each for 10 repetitions.*
- *Add 1 repetition per exercise each workout.*
- *Rest 3 minutes between exercises.*
- *Work through the list of exercises one time, top to bottom.*

Weeks 9–12

Three days per week

Two-hand swing
One-stays-up press
One-stays-up row
Single snatch
Double clean
Kettlebell back lunge
Chin-up (1 minute)
Push-up (1 minute)
Sit-up (1 minute)
Squat-pull

- *Perform one set each for 10 repetitions.*
- *Add 1 repetition per exercise each workout.*
- *Reduce repetitions by 20 percent in Week 12.*
- *Rest 3 minutes between exercises.*
- *Work through the list of exercises two times, top to bottom.*
- *Rest 3 minutes between cycles.*

Upon the completion of R&R, go back to Basic Training to begin a new training cycle. Keep a training log, and try to begin your new cycle at a slightly higher level than the same phase in the previous cycle. Also, when kettlebells are not available, try using sandbags instead. Not all of the kettlebell exercises will translate perfectly, but sandbags make a great, cost-effective substitution and work well in developing the same kind of functional strength as kettlebells do.

DRILLS FOR
INDIVIDUALS, TRAINING PARTNERS, AND TEAMS

16

Whether you train by yourself, with a partner, or with a team, you might want to spice up your workouts every once in a while. This section is meant to give you some ideas for creating drills to break up the monotony of long-term, intense training. Feel free to modify the drills to suit your needs.

Buffet Workouts: A Little Bit of Everything

A buffet workout is something you go through when you need a little time away from rigidly organized training. You might just be going into the off-season and are ready to work out but are not quite ready for too much structure. Two or three weeks of buffet workouts might be just what you need. If you are experienced in the nuances of strength and conditioning and know your body well, you can make a game of training. For example, on Day 1 you could allow yourself only one piece of equipment to train with, such as a 65-pound kettlebell. This means you would have to be creative in thinking up things that you could do with one fixed weight. Possibly one- and two-hand swings, squat-pulls, squat-presses, deadlifts, and duck-walks (two-handed carry). If you are strong, maybe single cleans, single snatches, and single presses, as well.

Another example of a buffet workout is to go and just play with the weights for as long as you feel like it. Your workout might consist of a handful of kettlebell exercises, as well as some more exhibition-oriented movements such as forward and backward kettlebell flips. Possibly set a number goal of 300 total squat-pulls, clean-presses, and flips. How you break up the total number of repetitions may vary from workout to workout.

Playing cards work as well. For Kettlebell Poker, either a predetermined number of cards or an entire deck is shuffled and dealt. The athlete is unaware of the order. An exercise is named, and the athlete must perform the number of repetitions stated on the first drawn card. Aces are worth 15; face cards are worth 10. If the athlete is unable to complete the set, the card gets placed back in the pile to be reused on another exercise. Whatever you decide, buffet workouts are meant to be fun and a way to give yourself a psychological break.

Killer Circuits

Circuit training is probably the most effective way to perform big strength and conditioning movements. It does not mean, however, that you will use light, single-joint exercises for a set time. Circuit training simply means that you will be running through your exercise list vertically instead of horizontally.

For example, instead of performing all of your sets of snatches, then going on to all of your presses and then all of your cleans, you perform one set of snatches, then one set of presses, and then one set of cleans. After the set of cleans, you start back at the top of the list. What this does is give you more time to recover between sets of the same exercise. You are able to reduce local muscular fatigue while still maintaining your desired training heart rate. This type of training is excellent for developing strength and power.

In the previous example, if you used a one-minute rest break between exercises, you would have only one minute between sets of snatches when the list was performed horizontally. If the list was performed vertically, you would have four or five minutes between sets of snatches. You would have more rest, be able to train more intensely, and still complete your total workload in the same amount of time.

Most of the sample workouts in this book are written to be performed in vertical fashion for this very reason. You can make the rest breaks as long or as short as you want. Also, you give the same priority to each exercise, instead of loading the beginning of the workout. For example, in horizontal fashion, if you were to perform all of your sets of snatches first, your back would be too fatigued to train your cleans intensely. If, however, you organized your training session in circuit fashion, you could perform your cleans with the same intensity as your snatches because you would avoid local fatigue by changing movements every set.

Killer circuits can be designed an infinite number of ways. They can be performed using only kettlebells or with odd implements such as sandbags, rocks, thick bars, dumbbells, barbells, or tires. The absolute best circuits, however, are a combination of all of the above.

Here are some samples to get you started. When you get the hang of it, you can be creative in making up some of your own. The weights and repetitions are only starting points and should be increased or decreased to your level.

SAMPLE 1

Single clean (115 lbs., 5 repetitions each side)
Stone carry (130-lb. stone, 20 yards)
Weight sled drag (150 lbs., 20 yards)
Tire flip (600 lbs., 20 yards)
Sprint (20 yards)

- *Go from one event into the next with no breaks.*
- *Without compromising technique, you are going for your best time.*
- *Rest as much as you need to; then go through it again for a total of three times.*

SAMPLE 2

Single clean (65 lbs., 15 repetitions each side)
Squat-pull (65 lbs., 20 repetitions)
Single snatch (65 lbs., 10 repetitions each side)
Squat-pull (65 lbs., 20 repetitions)
Single press (65 lbs., 15 repetitions each side)
Bent-over row (65 lbs., 15 repetitions each side)

- *Warm up extremely well for this workout.*
- *Do not rest between exercises.*
- *Work through the list of exercises five times, top to bottom.*
- *Rest 5 minutes between cycles.*

SAMPLE 3

Double snatch (65 lbs. each, 5 repetitions each side)
Chin-up (bodyweight, 10 repetitions)
2-inch-thick bar deadlift (prone grip) (225 lbs., 5 repetitions)
Steep-incline dumbbell press (90 lbs., 10 repetitions)

- *Rest 3 minutes between exercises.*
- *Work through the list of exercises three times, top to bottom.*
- *Rest 3 minutes between cycles.*

SAMPLE 4

Double snatch (65 lbs., 5 repetitions each side)
Double press (65 lbs., 5 repetitions each side)
Barbell squat (315 lbs., 5 repetitions)
Flat-bench dumbbell press (100 lbs. each side, 5 repetitions)
Double clean (80 lbs. each side, 5 repetitions)

- *Rest 3 minutes between exercises.*
- *Work through the list of exercises five times, top to bottom.*
- *Rest 5 minutes between cycles.*

Kettlebell Duals

A kettlebell dual is a type of partner drill. While one athlete is performing an exercise, the partner is either resting or jogging in place. You could train for a specific time or a specific number of repetitions. When training for time, set a goal of performing squat-pulls for 20 minutes, for example. Then perform a specific number of repetitions per set that will challenge but not exhaust you—10 works well. While you execute your set of 10 squat-pulls, your partner jogs in place; then you switch. Take turns until 20 minutes have passed.

You could also break things up by performing an exercise for 10 minutes and then switching to a different exercise such as single snatches. When training for a repetition goal, you and your partner can set a specific number goal for each of you or you can work toward a combined total. When training for a target number that is shared equally, you would again pick a specific repetition goal per set: again, 10 works well.

If you want to make this more of a competition, you can try to do as many repetitions per set as possible when it is your turn. Whoever reaches the target goal in the fewest number of sets wins. Another way to make a competition out of a workout is to train with a progressive number of repetitions per set. You do one, your partner does one; you do two, your partner does two; and so on. Whoever completes the set with the greatest number of repetitions wins.

Circle of Pain: The Becker Bucket

The circle of pain was created by my good friend Dr. Tom Connolly, a 5th Dan in Kodokan Judo. It is a team-building drill that is meant to motivate, not intimidate. Dr. Connolly, I, and fifteen to twenty of our friends, mostly high school and college athletes and martial artists, would get together on a weekend and go through a kettlebell workout that would last about three hours. We would divide into two to three groups based on size, body weight, or both. We would then get in line and each perform a set. Waiting in line was our rest break. It usually worked out to 3 to 5 minutes between sets.

Also, this was organized to progress horizontally, although a vertical progression would work as well. Everyone there was in pretty good shape to begin with, and we did these workouts only once every four weeks or so for motivation and camaraderie. They would look something like the following:

Squat-pull (145 lbs., 10 sets of 10)
Single clean (95 lbs., 5 sets of 5 repetitions each side)
Single snatch (65 lbs., 5 sets of 5 repetitions each side)
Bent-over row (65 lbs., 5 sets of 5 repetitions each side)
Single press (65 lbs., 5 sets of 5 repetitions each side)
Kettlebell push-up–row (65 lbs., 5 sets of 5 repetitions each side)
Double clean (65 lbs., 5 sets of 5 repetitions each side)
Alternating clean (65 lbs., 5 sets of 5 repetitions each side)
One-stays-up row (50 lbs., 3 sets of 10 repetitions each side)
One-stays-up press (50 lbs., 3 sets of 10 repetitions each side)

Then came the circle of pain (yes, this is G-rated). We would get into a circle and go through a sort of hot potato game with kettlebells. Every other lifter had a kettlebell of either 35, 50, or 65 pounds. If there was no one under 200 pounds of body weight, we would take out the 35-pound weights. People without weights jogged in place, and those with weights would perform 10 squat-pulls and then pass the kettlebell to their right. Jogging in place was the active rest, so the goal was to finish your set without slowing down or the kettlebells would pile up next to you and you would lose your active rest break.

We would set a timer for 20 minutes and go until it sounded. If someone quit (someone always quit), we would keep the weight in the circle and reduce the number of active rest breaks that the remaining lifters received. We were fueled by pride at this point.

What is the Becker Bucket you ask? By now I'm sure that you have figured out that the Becker Bucket was for someone who didn't quite make it through the workout or ate too much for breakfast. It was kept in the middle of the circle and was always named after the last lifter to use it, hence the name "Becker Bucket." It was a kind of badge of honor.

You and your friends can come up with your own version of the circle of pain. Twenty to thirty minutes works best. You can assign a leader and change the exercise each time one of the kettlebells makes it around the circle. Or you can simply keep the same exercise throughout. Try to build in an active rest period. Jumping jacks, jogging in place, body-weight squats, or even push-ups all make great active rest breaks. Also, any big, multi-joint kettlebell movement will work in the circle of pain. Of course, squat-pulls work, but sidewinders, two-hand swings, cleans, snatches, double cleans, double snatches, and so on will also work. You get the idea, and of course, don't forget your bucket!

Conclusion

At the End of the Day . . . Kettlebells

Whether it is to run a marathon or to be able to play with your grandkids, each of us has a goal that is personal and important. It doesn't matter how big you are, how old you are, or how much money you make; next to family and friends, our most valuable possession is our health. That being said, we all know that strength training for health or just daily living is an absolute necessity.

Society has become sedentary and automated. We drive everywhere, buy prepared food, and sit most of the day. We need to set aside a formal time to exercise because we would not get physical activity otherwise.

Now imagine your perfect workout. It might be something that allows you to run faster or give you more endurance. It might be something that gives you the ability to jump higher or punch harder. Or it might be just something that is time efficient and will keep you flexible and give you energy to do the things in life that are important to you. Whatever your goals, I say with absolute conviction that kettlebells can help you achieve them.

Kettlebells are versatile, time-tested implements. They have produced tremendous results for ages. True, they were temporarily out of favor—not because they lost their effectiveness, but because we as a society forgot how to work hard. It is obvious that we are coming to our senses because once again, kettlebells are back. At the end of the day, exercise theory can be reduced to simplicity, hard work, and kettlebells.

Index